"*Prayer On Fire* will be a book that will have a lasting impact on your life. Fred doesn't just write about fire, he craves, longs for, and lives the passion and intensity that fire brings. The church has confused the dust of human effort from the cloud of God's presence. You need to read this book."

— ALICE SMITH, executive director, U.S. Prayer Center,
www.usprayercenter.org

"*Prayer On Fire* is a wonderful explanation of how the Holy Spirit makes prayer happen in a person and in a church. My prayer life also used to be a duty, a 'flicker' in flame. Then the Holy Spirit touched me, and I could not pray enough. I am so thankful for this book's message and the fruit it will inspire in the church."

— DR. TERRY TEYKL, founder and director,
Renewal Ministries and the World Methodist Prayer Team

"Fred Hartley's book *Prayer On Fire* is a convicting, encouraging, challenging, Christ-exalting call to a basic long neglected by the West: prayer! If there is a spiritual fiber in your being, it will call you to passionately embrace renewed communion with God and drive away the mechanical routine of voicing but not praying the thoughts of your heart. It will revitalize your spiritual life. It's a must-read!"

— HAROLD J. SALA, PhD., author of *Touching God: 52 Guidelines for Personal Prayer*; founder and president, Guidelines International

"Fred Hartley has helped us connect with the transforming fire that represents the Holy Spirit's activity in our prayer life. This book will rekindle your longing for a passionate and life-altering prayer life that can move heaven into action."

— OS HILLMAN, president, Marketplace Leaders and
International Coalition of Workplace Ministries

D0289752

"We stand at the threshold of a nationwide Christ-awakening in answer to over two decades of united prayer across the land. In this remarkable book, Fred shapes our expectations about how this impending move of God will manifest itself, showing us ways to enter into it even now. The hope that springs from the last chapter is by itself worth the price of the book!"

—DAVID BRYANT, founder, PROCLAIM HOPE!; author of *Christ Is All!*

"Fred Hartley is one of the key prayer leaders that God has raised up for this generation, and *Prayer On Fire* is a powerful book with a life-affecting message for all of us."

—DR. PAUL CEDAR, chairman, Mission America Coalition

PRAYER ON FIRE

WHAT HAPPENS WHEN THE HOLY SPIRIT IGNITES YOUR PRAYERS

FRED A. HARTLEY III

NAVPRESS®

BRINGING TRUTH TO LIFE

A *Pray!* Magazine book
Pray! Books • P.O. Box 35004, Colorado Springs, CO 80935
www.praymag.com

OUR GUARANTEE TO YOU

We believe so strongly in the message of our books that we are making this quality guarantee to you. If for any reason you are disappointed with the content of this book, return the title page to us with your name and address and we will refund to you the list price of the book. To help us serve you better, please briefly describe why you were disappointed. Mail your refund request to: NavPress, P.O. Box 35002, Colorado Springs, CO 80935.

The Navigators is an international Christian organization. Our mission is to reach, disciple, and equip people to know Christ and to make Him known through successive generations. We envision multitudes of diverse people in the United States and every other nation who have a passionate love for Christ, live a lifestyle of sharing Christ's love, and multiply spiritual laborers among those without Christ.

NavPress is the publishing ministry of The Navigators. NavPress publications help believers learn biblical truth and apply what they learn to their lives and ministries. Our mission is to stimulate spiritual formation among our readers.

ISBN 1-57683-960-5

Cover design by Wes Youssi/The DesignWorks Group, Inc.
Cover image by IndexStock
Creative Team: Connie Willems, Amy Spencer, Arvid Wallen, Angie Messinger

Some of the anecdotal illustrations in this book are true to life and are included with the permission of the persons involved. All other illustrations are composites of real situations, and any resemblance to people living or dead is coincidental.

Unless otherwise identified, all Scripture quotations in this publication are taken from the HOLY BIBLE: NEW INTERNATIONAL VERSION (NIV). Copyright © 1973, 1978, 1984 by International Bible Society. Used by permission of Zondervan Publishing House. All rights reserved. Other versions used include: the *Revised Standard Version Bible* (RSV), copyright 1946, 1952, 1971, by the Division of Christian Education of the National Council of the Churches of Christ in the USA, used by permission, all rights reserved; and the *King James Version* (KJV).

Library of Congress Cataloging-in-Publication Data
Hartley, Fred A.
  Prayer on fire : what happens when the Holy Spirit ignites your prayers / Fred A. Hartley III.
     p. cm.
  Includes bibliographical references.
  ISBN 1-57683-960-5
  1. Prayer—Christianity. 2. Holy Spirit. I. Title.
  BV210.3.H375 2006
  248.3'2—dc22
                                        2006007017

Printed in the United States of America
1 2 3 4 5 6 / 10 09 08 07 06

FOR A FREE CATALOG OF NAVPRESS BOOKS & BIBLE STUDIES,
CALL 1-800-366-7788 (USA) OR 1-800-839-4769 (CANADA)

CONTENTS

To my
full-throttle,
wide-open,
passionate
friend and one and only son-in-law,
Josh
—God couldn't have given our daughter a
better life partner—
and to your generation of God-seekers,
who refuse to settle for less than prayer on fire.

INTRODUCTION

This book is all about fire.

I want to introduce you to the fire of God's tangibly manifest presence and show you what happens when this fire takes hold of our prayer lives.

This fire suddenly makes known the invisible God in unmistakable ways. It is a fire that will cleanse and restore; a fire of purity and passion and power; a fire that will rescue broken lives, rebuild marriages, and strengthen moral fiber. This fire starts in heaven and reveals the presence of the living God on earth.

The Bible is full of fire. Stories of people who met God in the fire are sprinkled from the first pages to the final chapters. In each example, God's people are led to a fresh encounter with God, and their prayer lives are revolutionized. Just consider some initial evidence.

- Abraham met God in the fire. His vision of the smoking firepot and a blazing torch convinced him that his love covenant with God was ratified.[1]
- Moses met God in the fire. He was changed in a day, when God spoke to him from the flaming bush.[2] Later he received the ten laws on a mountain covered with fire.[3]
- All Israel met God in the fire. They were led through the wilderness by a pillar of cloud by day and a pillar of fire at night.[4]
- David met God in the fire. One day, as he knelt before God in worship, the fire of God miraculously consumed his sacrifice.[5]

- Solomon met God in the fire. When he dedicated the temple with his hands raised to God in prayer, fire came from heaven and burned the offering. God's presence was so overwhelming that the priests were unable to perform their duties.[6]
- Elijah met God in the fire. When he challenged the prophets of Baal to a showdown at Mount Carmel, the fire of God consumed the sacrifice, the wood, the stones, and even the water in the trench.[7]
- Isaiah met God in the fire. He was never the same once the angel pressed a white-hot coal of God's holiness against his lips.[8]
- John the Baptizer met God in the fire. He announced, "I baptize you with water for repentance. But after me will come one who . . . will baptize you with the Holy Spirit and with fire."[9]
- The entire early church met God in the fire. On the day of Pentecost they were covered with what appeared to be flames of fire.[10]
- Paul met God in the fire. It was from a blinding flash of light that God said, "I am Jesus, whom you are persecuting."[11] Later, the apostle warned, "Do not put out the Spirit's fire."[12]
- John, on the Mediterranean island of Patmos, met God in the fire. When he saw the exalted Christ, his Lord was on fire from head to toe. Christ's eyes were like flames of fire, His feet glowed as in a furnace, and His face shone like the sun in all its brilliance.[13]
- The writer of the book of Hebrews met God in the fire. Point-blank he declared, "Our 'God is a consuming fire.'"[14]

In each of these examples, the God who is everywhere present and yet normally invisible suddenly and sovereignly chose to make known His breathtaking presence in ways that His people could understand.

Was God present with Moses prior to the burning bush? Certainly. But Moses was not conscious of God's presence until He spoke to him from the fire.

Was God present with Israel prior to the pillar of fire? Well, of course. But God did not reveal His presence until He appeared in the glory column and the fiery pillar.

Was God present with the early church prior to the flames of fire appearing on every believer's head on Pentecost? Most definitely. We would all agree there was no way the early church could demonstrate such unity of purpose in such a high-level prayer gathering without the work of the Holy Spirit. But it was not until the fire descended that God's presence became obvious to all.

As we will discover, God often uses fire to make Himself known. When He does, He empowers His people and expands His kingdom. It all starts with fire.

SEEKERS ON FIRE

I am encouraged to realize how many God-seekers in more recent days have met Him in the fire. Samuel Logan Brengle of the Salvation Army told of meeting God in the fire: "My soul melted like wax before fire."[15]

Oswald Chambers, author of the blockbuster devotional book *My Utmost for His Highest*, declared, "The Holy Spirit must anoint me for the work, fire me . . . nothing but the fire of the most Holy Spirit of God can make the offering holy and unblameable and acceptable in His Spirit."[16]

John Wesley said, "I felt my heart strangely warmed."[17]

Revivalist George Whitefield was known as "the fire-bringer."[18]

John Calvin called the entire church "the fellowship of the flaming heart."[19]

Missionary martyr Jim Elliot asked, "Am I ignitable, O God?"[20]

Charles Haddon Spurgeon was practically obsessed with fire. He referred to it a whopping 1,168 times in his sermons alone. On at least one occasion, he boldly exhorted pastors, "Your work, brethren, is to set your church on fire."[21] Again he proclaimed, "Keep up the fire within, and add fresh fuel to give a more fervent heat."[22] He sternly warned Christians against a lukewarm, indifferent relationship with the God of fire:

> The church of God is like fire, and you cannot say to fire, "You must burn comfortably at the corner of that haystack and never think of going any farther." "No," says the fire, "I will burn it all down." "But there are farm buildings yonder: do not touch those sheds and barns." The fierce fire is insatiable; it never stops while there is anything to be consumed.[23]

More recently, Jim Cymbala, pastor of the renowned Brooklyn Tabernacle in New York City, cried out in single-minded desperation, "Fill our churches with fresh wind and fresh fire!"[24]

These fire-seekers are not alone. We are becoming a people who are crying out for fresh fire from God. Nothing demonstrates this better than the vast number of new songs calling for fire. If you go online and look up contemporary Christian songs with the word *fire* in the title, you will discover at least six hundred songs. If you include those that contain *fire* in the lyrics, the number jumps into the thousands.

Songwriter Matt Redman expresses his heart's cry in "I Need to Get the Fire Back," in which he declares, "The embers still remain, but Lord I miss the flame."[25] David Crowder sings a Matt Redman song, "Let worship be the fuel for mission's flame."[26] The contemporary Christian band Shane and Shane sings, "Burn away the dross. Holy fire of God."[27] Tim Hughes wrote, "Consuming fire, fan into flame a passion for your name."[28] Charlie Hall sings, "Send us with fire to go love the world."[29] And Third Day sings, "Yes our God. He is a consuming fire and the flames burn down deep in our soul."[30] These lyrics represent only the tip of the flame. They speak of a raging inferno of passion for the reality of God's manifest presence. May this book fuel the same fire in you.

STEPPING INTO THE FIRE

As we step into the holy ground of your inner self and talk about developing an authentic, relevant prayer life where you welcome His presence into your everyday world, I want to make a few commitments to you.

I will be vulnerable. I am a fellow seeker with an intense passion to know Christ better. I have made plenty of mistakes and have wrestled with my lukewarm heart. I will roll up my sleeves and share what I've learned in my journey.

I will be biblical. I don't have all the answers, and I won't pretend to. The Bible, however, does provide answers, so we'll look at Scripture—and plenty of it.

I will be encouraging. Without apology I call you to seek Christ with all your heart—with the throttle wide open. While it is wrong to seek a particular experience with God, it is not wrong to seek an encounter with God. In fact, God loves it when we seek Him. There is only one way to seek Him and find Him and that is to seek Him with our whole heart.[31] My goal is to lead you to a fresh encounter with the white-hot presence of God.

I will be respectful. When it comes to Word-and-Spirit theology, there is a wide range of preferences. I will show respect and sensitivity to our various traditions. Before we are done, we will even discover that many of our traditions were actually born in the fire.

More than a manual or a textbook, this book is a manifesto. It is a rallying cry to experience a robust, relevant prayer life that will fill you with flaming wonder as you encounter the tangible presence of God. I want the fire of God's presence to burn in my life, in my local church family here in metro-Atlanta—and in your life. Allow me to introduce you to *prayer on fire*.

CHAPTER ONE

GOD ON FIRE

Sometimes we forget that God is fire.
We confuse him with fireplaces and fireworks.
ERWIN MCMANUS[1]

"Safe?" said Mr. Beaver; "don't you hear what Mrs. Beaver tells
you? Who said anything about Safe? 'Course he isn't safe.
But he's good. He's the King, I tell you."
C. S. LEWIS[2]

God is a consuming fire.
THE BIBLE[3]

rayer is what we do. It is our initiative to meet God, whether we are asking for favors, singing in celebration, or crying out in distress. Regardless of what shape or size it comes in, prayer is our effort to engage God.

Fire, on the other hand, is what God does. It is God's initiative to meet us. Fire comes when the self-revealing God chooses to give us a glimpse of His character, His activity, His purposes, or His presence. We experience fire when He takes the paper-thin membrane that separates heaven and earth in His hands and tears it from top to bottom, enabling us to look inside and giving us the privilege of seeing Him firsthand. Point-blank, *fire is the manifest presence of God.*

Because prayer is what we do, and fire is what God does, prayer on fire is what happens when what we do and what God does slam together. It is when God's initiative toward us meets our initiative toward Him. Prayer on fire happens when the Holy Spirit gets His hands on our prayers and turns our common, ho-hum, everyday lives into a showcase for His extraordinary presence. As we will discover, prayer on fire is what God-seekers have experienced throughout biblical and church history and right up to this present day.

DESIRE ON FIRE

Let's face it. Most of us are all too familiar with fireless prayer. How many times have I lamented, *If only I could fix my prayer life!* Yes, I want to see answers to prayer, but even more important, I want to know Christ. I want to know the reality of His presence in my daily prayer and worship times. Yet prayer has often made me feel like a loser. And I find I am not alone.

Although we are sincere, many of us have had it all backward when it comes to prayer. We are prone to start with what we do—our techniques, our postures, our patterns, our efforts, our self-discipline. We have tried to generate our own prayer lives. Consequently we are bone-tired and empty inside. Surely our prayers ought to be a source of refreshment, yet too often they have become a source of exhaustion.

A recent survey of more than a thousand pastors and Christian leaders from a broad spectrum of the body of Christ asked, "What is your greatest perceived need?" They gave an almost unanimous answer. The single need that stood far above all others was for consistent, passionate prayer. One leader lamented, "We do pretty much everything at church but pray. Our focus is horizontal, not vertical."[4] It is as if prayer has become the Achilles' heel of the modern church.

On one of his first audiotapes, "Managing Your Money," Larry Burkett told of a famous Chinese pastor who shared his gripping message in megachurches across the United States. At the end of this pastor's tour, his interpreter asked, "What impressed you most about the church in the United States?" He promptly replied, "The thing that impressed me most about the church in the United States is how much they can do without God." *Ouch!* I thought as I listened. The truth hurts.

Prayer without God's presence leaves us scrambling to see how much we can accomplish as we try to make up for what God is not doing. It is all too easy to conclude that fireless prayer is normal. This is tragic. Because this kind of prayer is all some of us have experienced, we have mistakenly concluded that it's all there is.

In many ways we are at a precipice. Will we settle for second-hand information about God, or will we rediscover prayer on fire and, thereby, come to know His tangible presence? We have heard the stories and read the books about mighty moves of God in the past, but have *we* been touched by the fire? It is not an overstatement to say we are currently experiencing a prayer crisis that is as serious as the AIDS epidemic in Africa. We recognize the need, but we don't know what to do about it. As AIDS attacks the body's immune system and makes it impossible to resist a simple virus, so fireless prayer leaves us anemic, vulnerable, and disease-ridden. Fireless prayer is the blight on the body of Christ today.

The word the Bible uses in the book of Revelation for fireless Christianity is *lukewarm*. This word picture from Jesus' message to the early church at Laodicea should work well in our Starbucks culture. "Serve us our coffee fresh, robust, full-bodied, and piping hot!" we request. Well, God doesn't like warmed-over people any more than we like a warmed-over brew. He wants our lives to be passionate, hot, aromatic, full-bodied. "Because you are lukewarm—neither hot nor cold—I am about to spit you out of my mouth," Jesus warned.[5]

The human spirit becomes lukewarm when it has not recently been exposed to the white-hot presence of the living God. It becomes lethargic, anemic, and bored. A lukewarm heart breeds listless worship, casual commitment, and duplicitous obedience. Fortunately God does not give up on the lukewarm. Instead He offers us a cure: a fresh encounter with the blazing presence of the risen Christ. In fact, He invites us to welcome His presence. "Here I am!" Jesus said, "I stand at the door and knock. If anyone hears my voice and opens the door, I will come in."[6] To put it another way, God's answer for the lukewarm heart is prayer on fire. It happens when God comes and manifests His presence to us.

SOULS ON FIRE

This afternoon I received an e-mail from one of my favorite people, Josh. He is my one and only son-in-law. "I have one request," he said in his typical straightforward manner. "Can you pray that the Lord would set me on fire?"

Yikes! I thought with admiration, *what a bold request!*

I paused, took a deep breath, and considered his words again. I thought of another huge request he had presented to me two years earlier: "May I have your daughter's hand in marriage?" (If you knew how protective I am, you would know how much guts that request required.) But he was asking for something that, I would dare say, is even bigger: He wanted me to ask God to set him on fire. You see, Josh is not interested in a mere intellectual understanding of fire. He doesn't want God to set his marriage on fire or his career on fire. That would be good, but he takes it one step further: He wants God to set *him* on fire.

"Pray that the Lord would set me on fire!" is one of those ultimate, no-turning-back requests. And it represents the heart cry of an increasing number of desperate God-seekers who are tired of mediocre prayers and lackluster worship.

What about you? Does your soul echo this desire for the fire of God's glorious presence to penetrate your life? Are you tired of lukewarm prayers? Are you hungry to know Christ better and better? If so, I have good news for you. If you are a Christ-seeker and desire a more relevant prayer life, God is already at work in you.

The Bible plainly says, "There is . . . no one who seeks God." It even says, "All have turned away. . . . There is no fear of God before their eyes."[7] This means that, left to ourselves, we lack the slightest motivation to pursue Christ. Therefore, if we *are* motivated to know Christ better, God is at work in us. Even if we are painfully aware of our ineffective prayers, the very fact that we want to do something about them shows the preliminary handiwork of God. In a sense, the desire for fire is the promise that fire will indeed follow. It's as if God takes the wood, hay, and stubble of our inadequate efforts to pursue Him and sets them on fire with His glorious presence. We may not yet see the fire of His presence, but at least there is smoke. And where there is smoke, you know what is about to happen!

Let me warn you at this point: Be careful not to confuse fire with a human emotion or with what is often called passion. Coaches tell their players to "fire up!" A romance novel talks about burning with passion. But as I use the term *fire,* I am not talking about excessive emotion or even honest, pure-hearted, spiritual passion. Such passion in the human soul *is* often the result of our spirits encountering the flaming presence of God's Spirit. The soul—made up of the mind, will, and emotions—does become zealous and passionate when it glows with the fire of God, but that will be the topic of another book. This book is not about our soul's passionate response;

it is about the Holy Spirit's passionate initiative. I am not in any way challenging you to rev your spiritual engines, crank up your emotional fervor, or work yourself into a fever pitch. God forbid!

So then, where does the fire that ignites our prayer lives come from?

THE SOURCE OF FIRE

Plain and simple, prayer on fire is the work of God the Holy Spirit. True prayer is not only the work of man; it is also the work of the Holy Spirit. The Bible often shows how the Holy Spirit is responsible for generating effective prayer.

At a watershed moment in their lives, the disciples caught Jesus praying. They were blown away to watch a man so skilled at His craft. Something about the way He prayed was so radically superior to anything they had seen in the other religious people that they immediately pleaded, "Lord, teach us to pray." Jesus grabbed the teachable moment with both hands, giving them a prayer pattern, a prayer picture, and some prayer promises.[8] But He saved the best till last. He didn't give them the real punch line until the end of His discourse: "If you then, though you are evil, know how to give good gifts to your children, how much more will your Father in heaven give the Holy Spirit to those who ask him!"[9]

In a sense Jesus answered, "Okay. You want to learn to pray? There is only one way. You must ask the Holy Spirit to come and teach you. He alone will make it possible for you to pray the way I do."[10]

The apostle Paul also understood Spirit-generated prayer. He knew that the only way he could get his prayers off the ground was with supernatural assistance. He was well acquainted with his inadequacies in prayer when he wrote, "We don't know how to pray as we ought." He went on to express that he was equally familiar with the incredible ability of God's indwelling Spirit to help with this chronic weakness: "but the Spirit himself intercedes for us."[11] It is no wonder that when Paul called Christians to prayer, he told them not to muster up their own prayers, but to "pray in the Spirit."[12]

The Holy Spirit is both a flaming Spirit and a praying Spirit. This means that if we have a problem with the relevance and authenticity of our prayer lives, the real problem is with our relationship with God the Holy Spirit. This pattern of Spirit-generated fire and Spirit-generated prayer is much more than a coincidence; it encapsulates the essence of a revolutionary principle that runs straight through the Bible: *All effective prayer is generated by God the Holy Spirit and leads us to a fresh encounter with God.*

GOD'S FIERY PRESENCE

The real scandal of lukewarm prayer is that it forfeits the knowledge of God. Don't get me wrong. I'm not suggesting that when we are lukewarm we lack all knowledge of Christ, but we do settle for a superficial acquaintance. The problem is complicated by the fact that we often fail to recognize the profound difference between God's everyday omnipresence and His manifest presence.

God's omnipresence—the fact that God is everywhere present—is celebrated in Psalm 139:7-8:

Where can I go from your Spirit?
Where can I flee from your presence?
If I go up to the heavens, you are there;
if I make my bed in the depths, you are there.

We don't need to pray for God's omnipresence; everyone on the planet is already experiencing it. What we want, however, is His *manifest* presence. And for that we must pray.

A. W. Tozer pointed out the distinction: "The Presence and the manifestation of the Presence are not the same. There can be one without the other. God is here when we are wholly unaware of it. He is manifest only when and as we are aware of His Presence."[13] Tozer borrowed this helpful distinction from the English Puritans and the German Pietists before them. Both the Puritans and the Pietists longed continually to experience God's life-transforming presence. In fact, if they did not encounter God tangibly, at times they would cancel all other church activities and devote themselves to focused corporate prayer, asking God to make Himself known conspicuously. They wanted to experience conviction of sin, repentance, purity, and the effects of walking in vibrant spiritual intimacy with the risen Christ.

This pursuit is worth the payoff. As Tozer pointed out, "If we cooperate with Him in loving obedience, God will manifest Himself to us, and that manifestation will be the difference between a nominal Christian life and life radiant with the light of His face."[14]

What makes this experience of God possible is God's passion to make Himself known to us. Without a rock-solid understanding of this aspect of God's character, even the most zealous seekers will eventually come to a screeching halt. God is even more eager to make Himself known than we are to know Him. As I have already noted, He was seeking us before we started seeking Him. Again, to quote our friend Tozer, "Our pursuit of God is successful just because He is forever seeking to manifest Himself to us."[15]

I was first introduced to God's manifest presence when a friend and I sought Him in prayer in a most unlikely place.

FIRE IN THE BASEMENT

I was listening to Bob Dylan music with my friend in his basement. We were talking about sports, school, God, and girls. All of a sudden he turned to me and said, "You wanna pray?"

Huh? I thought, *Pray?! Where did that come from? What a wild idea!*

"Sure, why not!" I replied. Before I knew what was happening, he was on his knees. I figured, *Why not? If we're going to pray, let's go for it!*

Before my knees could hit the floor, he started, "Jesus, You are so awesome! It's so cool that we can just talk to You like this." His eyes were closed, but he was smiling.

"Yeah, God," I jumped in, "we know You are right here with us; we just want to worship You right now."

"I love You so much, Jesus," my friend continued without missing a beat. "You are so much bigger than a rock star, so much more powerful than the president of the United States, so much more understanding than a parent, more helpful than a coach . . . "

"Jesus, You are more dependable than a girlfriend," I added. None of these thoughts had ever before come to our minds. They were fresh and real and alive. "God, You are awesome!"

Back and forth we prayed. Ideas were popping. There was nothing religious about our prayers; we were just talking to the One who knew us thoroughly and loved us passionately. We lost track of time. It seemed as if heaven stood wide open in front of us and we were able to look inside. We felt small, contrite, and humbled; yet at the same time privileged, honored, and invigorated.

Forty-five minutes later we got up off our knees and looked at each other with wide-eyed wonder. As we flopped on the couch, we took a deep breath and agreed that we had never experienced anything like that. Like moths drawn to the light, we had feasted our eyes on Jesus, deeply admiring His character, His virtues, His excellence.

I had previously said a thousand prayers, but this was *prayer on fire*. I had read my Bible and done what was expected of me as a Christian, but on that night Christ blew me away. I did not speak in an unknown language nor was I in some heightened emotional state. But for the first time in my life I caught a glimpse of the glory of God, and from that moment on I was branded. I have never since wanted to settle for anything less than the manifest presence of God.

SEEKING FIRE

The fire we encountered is more than a good idea or the latest novelty for a curious generation. As we will discover, God loves to reveal Himself to His seeking people.

Since high school I have been privileged to experience the fire of God's manifest presence hundreds of times. In my private prayer life, in my family, and in my public ministry, I have seen God dramatically show up. As pastor of a church in metro-Atlanta and president of the College of Prayer,[16] which trains pastors and Christian leaders on four continents in prayer on fire, I have learned firsthand how God makes Himself known. I have learned what fans the flame of God's holy presence and what quenches it. While I take my responsibilities as a teacher seriously, let me assure you that I cannot set your prayers on fire. I can't even set my own on fire. In fact, it would be entirely inappropriate for me to try. God is self-revealing, and only God the Holy Spirit can open the eyes of our hearts, ignite our spirits, and empower our prayers.

As with the early disciples, it is a watershed moment in our lives when we genuinely ask, "Lord, teach us to pray." Jesus answers our sincere request in much the same way He answered His first-century followers: He points us to the Person of the Holy Spirit. The better we get to know the Holy Spirit, the more relevant and effective our prayer lives will become. In the following pages, more than simply gaining information, we will discover that true prayer flows out of an intimate relationship with God.

ꙅ ꙅ ꙅ

Get ready to step into a different time zone. We will momentarily flash back three millennia to gain a fresh look at former God-seekers who stood on the holy ground of God's manifest presence as they learned firsthand about prayer on fire.

CHAPTER TWO

A BIBLICAL THEOLOGY OF FIRE

Just as Moses could not forsake the sight of the burning bush, so a nation cannot mistake the sight of a burning man!
LEONARD RAVENHILL[1]

Flame is the air which true Christian experience breathes. It feeds on fire; it can withstand anything, rather than a feeble flame; but when the surrounding atmosphere is frigid or lukewarm, it dies, chilled and starved to its vitals. True prayer must be a flame.
E. M. BOUNDS[2]

The sign of Christianity is not a cross, but a tongue of fire.
SAMUEL CHADWICK[3]

The Bible is full of fire. God's first act in creation was to gather together gasses and set them on fire by declaring, "Let there be light."[4] When all is said and done and the fat lady sings, God's final act will be accomplished with fire.[5] All history is thereby bracketed with the fire of God. It started with creative fire and it will end with consuming fire. As we will discover in this chapter, from the first pages of the Bible to the last chapters, people meet God in the flames of His transforming presence.

Before we dig in, allow me to paint a picture with you in it. I want you to envision your life being set on fire by God. Imagine falling in love with Jesus all over again. Spending extended time with Him is the highlight of your day. You enter God's living room and sit with Jesus, gazing in wonder and awe. Your heartbeat quickens. You can't help but smile. You read the Bible and it is alive. Fresh ideas are popping. At times while you're reading, it's as if you are looking into the face of God, beholding His character, His beauty, His virtue. At other times you seem to be looking into a mirror reflecting a crystal-clear image of yourself.

In the light of such intimacy, you suddenly realize that God has been reading your mail. *Oh no!* you panic, *I have been found. There is nowhere to hide!* Bone-crushing conviction sets in. Face to face with God's impeccable moral virtue, you shrink back, feeling like a dirty rotten scoundrel. In contrition you openly admit your failures and beg for His mercy. God responds. Instantly He floods your soul with His unconditional love, with the convincing awareness that there is nothing you could ever do to make Him love you less and there is nothing you could ever do to make Him love you more.

Before you even realize what has happened, the horror of *Oh no! There is nowhere to hide* changes into *Oh good! There's no need to hide.* In the act of seeking God, you realize He's been seeking you. While reading the Bible, you discover it's been reading you. You find God to be all He claims to be and yourself to be all you are intended to be.

You are filled with the hope that your life is changing for the good. Twisted, selfish attitudes and self-destructive habits are being rooted out, and for the first time you believe that the Christian life is actually doable. You feel empowered by a new confidence. Your prayers are alive. You receive a particular God-assignment that will impact your world.

Now imagine being part of a church family experiencing the same awe in God's tangible presence. He permeates your gatherings like the aroma of homemade bread. Friendships become vulnerable and transparent. People come out from hiding. Prayer meetings are standing room only. Relationships are healed. Lives are transformed. Your whole neighborhood stands up and takes notice. A lead story about your city in *USA Today* reports that crime and poverty are way down, prisons are vacant, industry is up, and churches are packed to the rafters.

You may be thinking, *Well, that all sounds good, but is it realistic? Could it ever happen to me? Could it really happen in my family and in my church?* Let me assure you that all of this—and so much more—is possible. It is what happens when God the Holy Spirit makes Christ known to His people. As I lay out the biblical theology of fire, we will see how this picture I have just painted is the normal result when God shows up. There is nothing unrealistic or super-spiritual about it.

Countless times in Bible days God revealed His flaming manifest presence to His people. Fasten your seat belt; let's take a look.

GOD ON FIRE

The Bible reveals our triune God—Father, Son, and Holy Spirit—on fire. God's being and His Word are frequently covered with flames.

God the Father On Fire

When the living God wants to communicate His presence tangibly to ordinary people like you and me, it is surprising how often He uses fire imagery. The well-respected German Bible scholar Gerhard

Kittel writes, "In almost all the Old Testament theophonies, fire appears as a way of representing the unapproachable sanctity and overpowering glory of Yahweh."[6]

Both the Old and the New Testaments declare, "God is a consuming fire."[7] When Moses dared to ascend the flaming mountain to receive God's ten laws, God's fire seemed to blaze out of control. Bright-yellow DANGER: KEEP OUT! tape was wrapped around every tree and stone. Lightning flashed. Thunder roared. The people trembled. "Mount Sinai was covered with smoke, because the LORD descended on it in fire. The smoke billowed up from it like smoke from a furnace, the whole mountain trembled violently, and the sound of the trumpet grew louder and louder."[8] The people were warned with bold letters: "Be careful that you do not go up the mountain or touch the foot of it. Whoever touches the mountain shall surely be put to death."[9] This was no weenie roast. It was a roaring inferno. The God of fire was showing Himself, and His people trembled in their boots.

As New Testament believers we realize that this Old Testament event is not a passé moment in a dispensational economy. The writer of the book of Hebrews makes permanent application to every believer: "Since we are receiving a kingdom that cannot be shaken, let us be thankful, and so worship God acceptably with reverence and awe, for our 'God is a consuming fire.'"[10]

God the Son On Fire

As we have discovered, fire is the manifest presence of God. It comes as no surprise then that Christ, who came as the embodiment of God,[11] is frequently revealed as being on fire. In fact, in the book of Revelation we see Jesus on fire from head to foot. His eyes flash like laser beams, His feet glow like molten bronze, His hands hold flaming embers, and His face beams like the noonday sun.[12]

When Christ declared, "I am the light of the world,"[13] essentially He said, "I am the fire of the world. I am the One who brings the illumination of true wisdom, the One who dispels spiritual darkness and ignorance, and the One who enables people to know the living and true God." The Bible says, "In him was life, and that life was the light of men."[14] Jesus is also the light of heaven. There will be no sun there because the knowledge of the glory of God in the face of Jesus Christ will be all the light we will need.[15] It is fair to say that heaven is filled with the fire of God's manifest presence.

John the Baptizer saw in Jesus the ability to lead people into an encounter with the fire of God's tangible presence: "I baptize you with water for repentance. But after me will come one who is more powerful than I, whose sandals I am not fit to carry. He will baptize you with the Holy Spirit and with fire."[16] What a fitting summary of Jesus' ministry! It is obvious from the Baptizer's description that he anticipated Jesus administering this baptism of fire not to a select few but to all His followers—including you and me.

God the Holy Spirit On Fire

It is remarkable how often fire is used in the Bible to describe both the Person of the Holy Spirit and His activity. It was promised that Jesus would "baptize you with the Holy Spirit and with fire," and on the day of Pentecost, God no sooner poured out His Spirit on the praying believers than they were covered with what appeared to be flaming headbands.[17]

The apostle Paul warned, "Do not put out the Spirit's fire."[18] This strong statement presupposes that the ongoing fire of God's Spirit is already active within the life of every believer. We do not need to earn it, beg God for it, or somehow fan it into flame through our own effort. The Holy Spirit is already stoking the fire of His presence in each of our lives. At the same time, I must quickly add that this verse reminds us of the grave reality that it is possible for any of us to extinguish God's fire and refuse to obey the Holy Spirit's daily promptings.

God's Word On Fire

Not only is God on fire, but when He speaks, His words are like flames of fire. The prophet Jeremiah used the word *fire* forty-two times: thirty-eight times in the book that bears his name and four times in Lamentations. He wrote, "'Is not my word like fire,' declares the LORD."[19] He described the effect that God's words had on him as like fire burning in his bones.[20] When he preached, it was as if the Word of God came from his mouth like flames shooting from a propane torch.[21]

The Bible is full of others who met God in His flaming Word. Ezekiel could be called "the prophet of fire," because he used *fire* forty-five times. He, like Isaiah, received his call in the fire.[22] He saw fire between the wheels, fire in the house, fire on stones, fire in Egypt, fire in Zoan, and fire in Magog.[23] Because these prophets each declared, "Thus says the LORD," it is no surprise they would know firsthand the fire of God's tangible presence.

The other prophets' messages are peppered with fire as well. Daniel saw God's eyes like fire.[24] Hosea saw God's coming inferno.[25] Joel saw God's fiery presence before and behind God's people, hemming them in on every side.[26] The short book of Amos uses the word *fire* nine times, predominantly referring to God's radical day of reckoning. Obadiah saw God's fire in the middle of His people.[27] Micah saw the mountains melt like wax before God's fire.[28] Nahum saw God's fiery reckoning.[29] Zephaniah saw the fire of God's jealousy.[30] Zechariah identified the link between the manifest presence of God's fire like a surrounding blazing wall, and the revelation of God's glory within.[31] Malachi compared God to the refiner's fire used to purge, purify, and strengthen metals.[32]

As we move into the New Testament we hear two disciples say, "Were not our hearts burning within us while he talked with us on the road and opened the Scriptures to us?"[33] Jesus had just finished giving them a crash course on the Old Testament Christ.[34] As they listened, they experienced an internal nuclear meltdown as they glimpsed Christ revealed in the Bible.

Now that we have surveyed the biblical explanation of God's flaming presence, we want to zoom in on some of the specific ways God's people encounter Him in the fire.

GOD'S PEOPLE ON FIRE

The church was born in the fire, and it was born in prayer. The book of Acts carefully documents the birthing process. All the believers were praying together when "they saw what seemed to be tongues of fire that separated and came to rest on each of them. All of them were filled with the Holy Spirit and began to speak in other tongues as the Spirit enabled them."[35] Because we as the church were born in the fire, the flame of God's manifest presence is deeply embedded in our DNA.

What happens when we are on fire with Jesus' presence?

Conviction of Sin

When God's people are initially introduced to His blazing manifest presence, they normally fall on their faces, come under bone-crushing conviction of sin, or disintegrate.[36] One thing is sure: Their lives are never again the same. To explore just one biblical example of an individual who disintegrated in God's blazing presence, let's investigate the prophet Isaiah.

In the beginning of his book, Isaiah described his call to follow and serve God.[37] "I saw the Lord seated on a throne, high and exalted," he said, "and the train of his robe filled the temple." The muscle-bound angels screamed "Holy, holy, holy is the LORD Almighty; the whole earth is full of his glory" at such a decibel that the doorposts rattled, the bedrock cracked, and the temple where Isaiah was praying was suddenly filled with smoke. When he saw the molten lava of God's all-consuming holiness, he started to unravel. "Woe to me!" he cried. "I am ruined! For I am a man of unclean lips, and I live among a people of unclean lips, and my eyes have seen the King, the LORD Almighty."

Literally, Isaiah yelled, "I am disintegrating." Who wouldn't suffer a meltdown when confronting God's manifest presence? In response to Isaiah's repentance and open confession of sin, "then one of the seraphs flew to me with a live coal in his hand, which he had taken with tongs from the altar. With it he touched my mouth and said, 'See, this has touched your lips; your guilt is taken away and your sin atoned for.'"

Is it any wonder that spontaneous combustion would take place inside Isaiah's soul? He not only encountered the flaming coal of God's holiness, the fire touching his lips forever changed him. It is not surprising that after encountering God like that, Isaiah used the word *fire* thirty-four times in his prophetic book. He went on to predict that the Lord will come with fire and that everyone will one day recognize Him as a consuming fire.[38]

Kittel suggests using *Fire* as a name for Yahweh because it "denotes the majestic being of God embracing both grace and judgment simultaneously."[39] Numerous other Bible references to fire demonstrate the cleansing effect of God's manifest presence.[40] It is impossible to get intimate with God without experiencing a similar purging process.

Prayer

Once the sin within us is effectively dealt with, God welcomes us into a level of intimacy with Him we never dreamed possible and our prayer lives blossom. We see an example of this in how God met with Moses.

God gave Moses explicit details for setting up the Tent of Meeting. This was, after all, the place where Israel would encounter God.[41] He mandated, "The fire on the altar must be kept burning; it must not go out."[42] The permanent presence of fire was a critical element of the Tent of Meeting. The perpetual flame vividly communicated God's purifying, penetrating, passionate presence with the people.

Not only did God mandate fire on the altar, He also instructed Aaron to burn incense every morning and evening "so incense will burn regularly before the LORD for the generations to come."[43] Bible scholars suggest that the smoke of the fires was a constant reminder of the rising prayers of God's people, ever ascending before their Lord.[44] This is a vivid picture of prayer on fire. David echoed this picture when he prayed, "May my prayer be set before you like incense; may the lifting up of my hands be like the evening sacrifice."[45]

The New Testament also refers to the incense of prayer that rises continuously before God. When John glimpsed heaven in the book of Revelation, he saw "golden bowls full of incense, which are the prayers of the saints."[46] Like our prayers, incense is flammable but not self-combustible. Just as incense requires fire to burn, so prayer requires the Holy Spirit to penetrate God's presence and rouse His attention. These Spirit-combustible prayers are guarded in golden bowls in heaven until just the right moment when God will take hold of those bowls and toss them back down on the earth as reverse thunder.[47]

Empowerment for Service

Another aspect of encountering God's presence is that we are empowered to serve Him. Many great leaders were launched on a world-impact mission by the flaming God. The who's-who of notable fire-encounters includes Abraham, Moses,[48] David, Solomon, Isaiah, and Ezekiel,[49] to mention only a few. But the trump card is seen in the Upper Room where God's blazing presence transformed the early disciples.[50]

The most far-reaching mission ever launched was on the line. Essentially Jesus had said, "You will go into all the world and make disciples of all nations, but first stay and pray. As you pray I will clothe you with the fire of my fullness. Then I will launch you with supernatural booster rockets into history-shaping ministry."[51] For ten solid days, the 120 believers joined together in concerted, focused prayer.[52] Like children appealing to their father about a promise he had made, they persistently reminded God what Jesus had guaranteed them.[53]

It is reported that at Kennedy Space Center there is a single, enormous launching pad (Launch Complex 39) from which all space shuttles take off. The disciples knelt on a similar launching pad. Jesus promised them a significant mission and a sizable payload, saying, "You will receive power when the Holy Spirit comes on you; and you will be my witnesses in Jerusalem, and in all Judea and Samaria, and to the ends of the earth."[54]

Ten. Nine. Eight. "They all joined together constantly in prayer."[55] Seven. Six. Five. *We have ignition!* Four. Three. Two. One. "Suddenly a sound like the blowing of a violent wind came from heaven and filled the whole house where they were sitting."[56] *We have liftoff!* The early church met God in the fire, and they were launched into world-transforming ministry.

Instantly the fire of God's presence drew a crowd. Because of the feast of Pentecost, "there were staying in Jerusalem God-fearing Jews from every nation under heaven."[57] There were people from as far as Cappadocia and Pontus nine hundred miles to the north, from Libya twelve hundred miles to the south in Africa, from Arabia one thousand miles to the east, and from Rome to the west.[58]

Peter was empowered to preach powerfully to them because of the Holy Spirit's fire. Previously he had been a fearful and defeated man who had distanced himself from Christ by denying his Master three times. Now he proclaimed God's Word in a way that penetrated people's hearts as if he were wielding a flame-thrower. In God's cleansing presence, the crowd was cut to the heart and cried out, "What shall we do?" Peter's answer was straightforward: "Repent and be baptized, every one of you, in the name of Jesus Christ for the forgiveness of your sins. And you will receive the gift of the Holy Spirit."[59] On that day, three thousand people converted to Christ, were baptized, and received the Holy Spirit.

The empowerment for mission came because of the fire of God's manifest presence. Immediately Peter made it clear that the promise of Holy Spirit fire was not for a single, isolated dispensation, but rather for all generations, including our own. "The promise is for you and your children and for all who are far off," he proclaimed, "for all whom the Lord our God will call."[60] All God's people would now bear His flame.

Flame Bearing

The seven historic churches addressed in the book of the Revelation are each identified by the word picture of a lampstand,[61] or, more accurately, *flame-bearer*. It was not the lampstand's responsibility to produce the flame but simply to carry it permanently so that it gave light to all in the house. Similarly every local church is assigned the distinct role to be a flame-bearer of God's manifest presence.

One of the ways God enables us to carry His flame into the world is through what the Bible calls "manifestation gifts." The apostle Paul told the Christians in Corinth, Greece, "Now to each one the manifestation of the Spirit is given for the common good."[62] The widely respected lexicon of Bauer, Arndt, and Gingrich defines *phanerosis*, the Greek word translated here as "manifestation," as "something openly, publicly disclosed; to reveal the true, distinct identity of someone."[63]

Listed among these gifts that disclose the presence of God are prophecy, tongues and interpretations, words of wisdom and knowledge, faith, healings and other miracles, and distinguishing of spirits. Any gift can certainly be abused, and these manifestation gifts are no exception. However, when they are used appropriately with love and wisdom, they openly display the presence of God among His people and reveal His true and distinct identity.

These gifts are occasionally viewed as the more demonstrative gifts. While some evangelicals may gravitate toward the motivational gifts mentioned in Romans 12, if we want to embrace the fire of God's presence we certainly can't distance ourselves from the gifts described in 1 Corinthians 12. They are tangible means through which the church is intended to experience and carry God's manifest presence as bearers of His flame.

Jesus told His followers, "You are the light of the world. A city on a hill cannot be hidden. . . . In the same way, let your light shine before men, that they may see your good deeds and praise your Father in heaven."[64] Allow me to restate those familiar words: *You are fire-carriers in your generation. As you allow Me to manifest My presence in your daily life, it will be obvious to all that your lifestyle reflects My character. When they recognize My presence in you, they will praise your Father in heaven.* Jesus expects fire to be a way of life for all of us.

LIVES ON FIRE

Congratulations—you made it! The ride through the Bible's description of God's flaming presence is over. You may unbuckle your seat belt and reflect for a moment.

Now that we have surveyed the biblical theology of fire, seeing how God has revealed Himself in the fire and how God's people have been transformed as they encountered Him, perhaps something is stirring in your own soul. Perhaps you desire to know God better so that the picture I painted at the outset of the chapter begins to actually take shape in your life.

It is one thing to see the fire of God's presence leaping from the pages of our Bibles and yet another to see that same fire ignite our daily lives. In the next chapter we come eyeball-to-eyeball with the One who takes these biblical principles and moves them beyond theory to living reality. Allow me to introduce you to the Person of the Holy Spirit.

CHAPTER THREE

HOLY SPIRIT FIRE

The greatest need today is for men and women who know Jesus Christ as Savior to be filled with the Holy Spirit. If we are not filled with the Holy Spirit, we are sinning against God.
BILLY GRAHAM

The one thing needful for the church, and the thing which, above all others, men ought everywhere to seek for with one accord and with their whole heart, is to be filled with the Spirit of God.
ANDREW MURRAY[1]

The Holy Spirit is worth getting to know. In fact, He wants us to know Him intimately. If we want an authentic prayer life, a casual acquaintance will not cut it. A distant theoretical approach just won't do. Even this book might seem fascinating or conceptually stimulating, but the principles will never take hold in our lives until we cultivate a genuine friendship with the Spirit.

It would be helpful right now to take a crash course in the Person and work of the Holy Spirit. After all, this is one of the most confusing and controversial pieces of our theology.

I remember attending a high-school Bible study as a young believer. My youth pastor asked, "When you think of the Holy Spirit, what comes to mind?" The question seemed innocent enough.

I raised my hand and blurted out, "The Wizard of Oz!" He

looked back at me in shock. I tried to backpedal. "Well, you know, kind of a huge energy field or a nuclear power plant. Electricity! You know." My teacher wasn't buying it. His mouth hung open. *Oh, no!* I thought. *Did I say something wrong?*

Then a friend jumped in. "Isn't it sort of like Casper the Friendly Ghost? You know—Holy Ghost, Friendly Ghost." What had seemed to be a perfectly harmless question had suddenly erupted into a theological free-for-all. Needless to say, that was not quite what my youth pastor had in mind. I'm not sure he ever got that Bible study back on track.

The sincere, though misguided, answers my friend and I gave represent some of the confusion about the Holy Spirit Christians still encounter. Let's enroll in "Holy Spirit 101" to make sure we are on the same page.

HOLY SPIRIT 101

What comes to your mind when you think about the Holy Spirit? It will be helpful to identify seven facts about Him.

1. The Holy Spirit Is Fire.

As we investigate fire from a biblical perspective, we quickly recognize that every time the fire of God's manifest presence appears, the Holy Spirit is close at hand. As we saw in the previous chapter, the Spirit and fire often appear side by side in Scripture.

- "He [Jesus] will baptize you with the Holy Spirit and with fire."[2]
- "Do not put out the Spirit's fire."[3]
- God pours out His Holy Spirit on the day of Pentecost, and the believers are covered with fire.[4]

It is only logical that the Spirit and fire frequently appear together. Fire is the manifest presence of God, and the Spirit's primary function is to make God known. When God manifests His presence, the invisible, omnipresent God gives us eyes to see Him. He gives us this ability through the work of the Holy Spirit. We can accurately say that there has never been a person touched by the flaming presence of God apart from the work of the Holy Spirit.

2. The Holy Spirit Is a Person.

There is perhaps no more common misconception regarding the Holy Spirit than to regard Him as an impersonal force or an energy field. This was my perspective when my youth pastor asked his question. Yet nothing is more damaging to an intimate relationship with the Holy Sprit than to treat Him like something impersonal.

What makes the Spirit's Personhood even harder to understand is the wide range of word pictures used in the Bible to refer to Him. He is shown as a dove, water, breath, and of course, fire.[5] All of these words provide us with insight into the Holy Spirit, and yet none of them are personal. On the other hand, the other two Persons of the Godhead—the Father and the Son—are referred to by distinctly personal names.

Yet the Holy Spirit is indeed a Person. Consider the following descriptions that clearly identify His personhood:

- The Spirit has feelings. He feels affection, sadness, and even rejection.[6]
- The Spirit has a will. He gives gifts to those He chooses. He speaks; He rebukes, corrects, and guides; He commands; and He leads.[7]
- The Spirit has thoughts. He teaches, He witnesses, He prays, and He searches.[8]
- The Spirit has desires. He calls people into service, and He convicts and convinces.[9]

In addition, the Holy Spirit is referred to by the personal pronoun "He."[10] This may not sound terribly significant until we realize that in New Testament Greek, *spirit* is a neuter noun that would normally call for the impersonal pronoun *it*. If the Holy Spirit were not a person, it would have been far easier for the New Testament writers to have remained consistent with Greek vocabulary and use the impersonal pronoun. However, they broke from the normal Greek pattern and intentionally identified the Spirit with the distinctly personal *He*. He, the Holy Spirit, is just as much a Person as God the Father and God the Son.

And though He is a fire, in this case the fire is a Person. R. A. Torrey understood this important distinction: "It is impossible to rightly understand the work of the Holy Spirit, or to get into right relation with the Holy Spirit Himself and thus know His blessed work in our own souls, without first coming to know the Holy Spirit as a Person."[11]

3. The Holy Spirit Is a Divine Person.

There is one God who eternally exists in three Persons—Father, Son, and Holy Spirit—and each Person is fully equal in divine essence. God the Holy Spirit is just as much God as the Father and the Son. He doesn't take a back seat nor does He lack any divine attributes, divine honors, or divine activities.

The creation of the universe was a team effort. The Father spoke, the Word went out, and the Spirit hovered over the surface of the deep.[12] The Incarnation was a team effort as well. The Father sent the Son, and the Spirit overshadowed Mary, resulting in pregnancy and the incarnation of Christ.[13] When we see the Father, Son, and Holy Spirit, we always see three Persons—one God always operating in open communication and in perfect unity.

4. The Holy Spirit Is the Indwelling Person.

When we receive Christ as Savior, He enters every life by virtue of the Holy Spirit. Christ has a glorified, physical body and is currently at the right hand of God the Father in heaven. It is the Holy Spirit whom Christ has sent to live inside us. "If anyone does not have the Spirit of Christ," the apostle Paul said, "he does not belong to Christ."[14] When the Bible says, "It is God who works in you to will and to act according to his good purpose,"[15] that work is being done by the Spirit.

5. The Holy Spirit Is a Praying Spirit.

The apostle Paul knew that the only way he could get his prayers off the ground was with supernatural assistance. "The Spirit helps us in our weaknesses," he said. "We do not know what we ought to pray for, but the Spirit himself intercedes for us with groans that words cannot express."[16] He advised believers to "pray in the Spirit."[17] Rather than praying under our own influence, we are to pray under the influence of the Holy Spirit. To be filled with the Spirit is to be filled with prayer. Norwegian theologian O. Hallesby understood this principle from experience and said, "It is written that the Lord will pour out the Spirit of prayer. You need not then work yourself up into the spirit and attitude of prayer."[18]

6. The Holy Spirit Is an Invisible Person.

Because He is Spirit, He is not visible to the human eye. When Christians get cut, they do not bleed Holy Spirit. If we are X-rayed, the Holy Spirit will not show up on the film. Jesus compared the Holy Spirit to the invisible wind: "The wind blows wherever it pleases. You hear its sound, but you cannot tell where it comes from or where it is going."[19] As Leonard Ravenhill wrote, "Nature's two greatest forces are fire and wind, and these two were wedded on the day of Pentecost."[20]

This point may seem self-evident, but it is important to note. Because the Holy Spirit is invisible, He is easily overlooked or even mistreated. The Holy Spirit has lived inside us from the moment we received Jesus, and yet the sad fact is that some of us have yet to get to know Him.

Now let's put it all together before we move on to our final insight. The Holy Spirit is a Person with all the qualities of a person. He has feelings and a will. He thinks His own thoughts, has His own desires, makes His own decisions. He is fully God in every way. He is, in fact, the Person of the Godhead who lives invisibly inside every genuine Christian. Because He is a praying Spirit, He seeks to help us with our daily prayers. You and I are constantly relating to Him in one way or another. At times we bring Him pleasure by hearing His voice, seeking His heart, and following His lead. At other times, we make Him sad by doing things He has clearly warned us against. We can throw water on His fire by failing to do what He wants, or we can fan the flame of His presence by obeying Him.

Okay. We have gained some insight into who the Holy Spirit is. Now we want to discover what He does.

7. The Holy Spirit Is the Flaming, Indwelling, Invisible, Divine, Praying Person Whose Primary Objective Is to Make Jesus Known.

Jesus said about the Holy Spirit, "He will testify about me," and "He will bring glory to me by taking from what is mine and making it known to you."[21] Make no mistake; this role was not given to the Spirit as an afterthought. Nor was this a temporary assignment that the Spirit would only fulfill for a season. It has always been the Spirit's job to make God in Christ known to God's people.

Respected Bible teacher F. B. Meyer affirmed this primary role of the Holy Spirit: "He is like a shaft of light that falls on the Beloved Face, so that as in the photograph, you do not think about the light, nor the origin of the light, but you think about the face that it reveals." The Beloved Face that he refers to is, of course, the face of

Jesus. It is the Holy Spirit who drew us initially to Christ. It is the Holy Spirit who opened our hearts to Christ and who came to live inside us when we received Christ. It is the Holy Spirit who keeps us seeking hard after Christ so that every day we are falling more deeply in love with Christ. It is the Holy Spirit who opens the eyes of our hearts that we might see the riches we have in Christ. The Holy Spirit's role in each of us is to lead us to encounter daily the manifest presence of God. To state it another way, the Holy Spirit brings fire.

The fact that the Holy Spirit continually seeks to exalt Christ is linked to the fact that He is also constantly generating prayer inside us. Obviously the more clearly we see Jesus, the more fervently and effectively we will pray. This is where the streams of prayer and fire merge.

"BE FILLED"

It is impossible to do justice to the Person and work of the Holy Spirit without talking about fullness. From the moment we receive the Person of the Holy Spirit when we are born again, He has one method of operation: to saturate our lives. "Do not get drunk on wine," Paul wrote to believers. "Instead, be filled with the Spirit."[22]

In this context, being filled with the Spirit refers to being under His influence. While the Spirit comes to dwell in every Christian at the time of salvation, not every Christian is necessarily filled with the Holy Spirit. However, God's desire is "that you may be filled to the measure of all the fullness of God."[23] "For in Christ all the fullness of the Deity lives in bodily form," Paul said, "and you have been given fullness in Christ, who is the head over every power and authority."[24] That fullness is given to us through the Holy Spirit.

To be filled with the Spirit is to be saturated with the Spirit. This means that God permeates every cell in our bodies, influencing every relationship, controlling every thought, governing every member of our physical bodies, and transforming every area of our lives.

Some of us may start to distance ourselves at this point because the fullness of the Holy Spirit has long carried with it a stigma of emotionalism and excess. This often conjures up images of all kinds of wild behavior. We don't want to associate with anything that might bring disgrace to God's name. And rightly so. Yet we might be so afraid of false fire or misfire or backfire that we distance ourselves even from holy fire. There is no need to do so.

It is reasonable to assume that because the Holy Spirit is the indwelling, divine Person we can trust Him. Remember: the Holy Spirit is God. When we encounter Him we encounter all there is in God, including His love, kindness, mercy, truth, and compassion. For this reason we do not hold the Spirit at arm's length. We want to treat Him as our best Friend and closest Companion. We want to embrace all of His activity in our lives.

To be filled with the Holy Spirit embraces all He has for us so that He has unhindered and unrivaled dominion over us. He wants to remove any vestige of rival loyalties or alien authorities. The Spirit wants nothing less than to stamp *Jesus is Lord!* on every square inch of our lives so that we have one Lord, one purpose, one calling, and one loyalty. As someone once said, from the moment the Holy Spirit moves in, He does not simply want to be resident, he wants to be president.

THE STORY OF A FELLOW SEEKER

Allow me to risk rolling up my sleeves and sharing a very personal story of a breakthrough moment in my own journey. While I was in college, an African-American woman in my church outside of Chicago told me, "Fred, I's a prayin' for you." I genuinely thanked her—I needed all the prayer I could get.

The next Sunday, smiling from ear to ear, she repeated her

greeting: "Fred, I's a prayin' for you." Every Sunday she greeted me with the same words and the same biggie-sized smile. The gleam in her eye seemed to say, *I know something you don't know.*

One Sunday after her usual greeting I asked, "What are you praying for?"

"That you receive the gift!" she said with an even bigger smile.

"Oh, you mean the gift of the Holy Spirit and the gift of tongues," I answered. Her twinkling eyes confirmed my hunch. "Well, I already have the Holy Spirit," I smugly stated, "and I don't believe every Christian is necessarily given the gift of tongues, but thanks for praying for me." My answer satisfied me, but obviously did not satisfy her.

She would not be dissuaded. She just smiled with eyes twinkling even brighter and stated emphatically, "Fred, I's a prayin' for you!"

This continued week after week until I'd had enough. It was time to take the offensive. "Ma'am, thank you for praying, but I already have the Holy Spirit!"

She just smiled back and replied, "But does the Holy Spirit have you?"

BONG! That one hit me upside my theological head and left my ears ringing. Soon she began calling my home. "Fred, I's a prayin' for you." Her persistence started to make me angry. I had my pat theological answer, and I didn't want to be bothered by some overzealous woman.

"Ma'am, please. I'm glad you are praying for me," I said with an attitude, "but if you don't mind, please stop calling me." Even though we were on the phone, I knew she was smiling, and that bothered me even more.

"Fred," she asked, "if you's right and I's wrong, then how come you's the one all upset?"

BONG! BONG! She got me again. Her simple, straightforward logic broke through my arrogant avoidance. That night we came to an agreement. I told her I would read anything she recommended, and she agreed not to call me anymore. She'd just pray. The next week I even enrolled in an independent study project at Wheaton College on the Person and work of the Holy Spirit.

During the next three months I read over twenty-six hundred pages on the Holy Spirit. For starters, I read through the entire Bible. Then I read Augustine, Calvin, Luther, Owens, Franke, Wesley, Barth, and other notable theologians. I read devotional writers including R. A. Torrey, D. L. Moody, and Raymond Edman. I also read a few charismatic writers such as Merlin Carothers and Don Basham. I benefited from most and weeded out a few. In the process of my reading I came to certain life-changing conclusions:

- Yes. Every Christian has the Holy Spirit.[25]
- No. Every Christian is not necessarily filled with the Holy Spirit.[26]
- It is unequivocally God's will for every Christian to be filled with the Holy Spirit.[27]
- The Holy Spirit filled every believer on the day of Pentecost and it is His unrelenting desire to fill every Christian today.[28]
- Just as God wants us to receive eternal life by faith in Christ and not by feeling, so also He wants us to receive the infilling of the Holy Spirit by faith and not by feeling.[29]
- It is wrong to seek an experience, but it is certainly not wrong to seek an encounter with God. Seeking God as a thirsty deer seeks for the brook is evidence of real spiritual health.[30]
- Those who are hungry and thirsty for righteousness are the ones who will be filled.[31]
- The fullness of the Holy Spirit is given to empower us for both personal holiness and Christian service.[32]

- To be filled with the Holy Spirit is not something I do to myself; it's something God does to me. I am not filled with the Spirit because I become more committed or muster up more passion. I am filled, however, when I receive God's transforming work in me.
- God wants every believer initially to receive the filling of the Holy Spirit at one point in time, and He wants every believer continually to receive fillings. God calls for both what might be called a crisis (one-point-in-time) filling and an ongoing, daily, progressive filling of the Holy Spirit. The apostle Paul's statement "Be filled with the Spirit"[33] literally meant "be being filled" or "be perpetually in the state of being filled."
- And just as God wants us to know for certain that we have eternal life, so He wants us to know for certain that we have received the filling of the Holy Spirit.[34]

As I diligently studied, and as my prayer-partner interceded for me, I became honest with myself and objective about the material I was considering. I had to admit that my soul was tired and weary. I was tired of dry Bible reading, forced spiritual disciplines, and lukewarm prayer. I had surrendered my life to Christ a thousand times, but inside I was fatigued. At the same time, I was deep-down hungry for God. I knew there was so much more of Jesus yet to discover, and I wanted all of Him.

My crisis moment came on a Saturday morning. That day I finally claimed by faith the promise of the filling of the Holy Spirit.

I read a string of Bible verses that boosted my faith to receive the Spirit's fullness: "'If anyone is thirsty, let him come to me and drink. Whoever believes in me, as the Scripture has said, streams of living water will flow from within him.' By this he meant the Spirit."[35] I was certainly thirsty, so I figured I qualified.

"Do not get drunk on wine. . . . Instead, be filled with the

Spirit."[36] Being filled is not some luxury for a few elite believers; it is the will of God for all of us. God commands it. To settle for less would be disobedient.

"If you then, though you are evil, know how to give good gifts to your children, how much more will your Father in heaven give the Holy Spirit to those who ask him!"[37] This verse gave me all the permission I needed, not only to ask but also to receive.

"But you will receive power when the Holy Spirit comes on you; and you will be my witnesses."[38] I sure needed power; I was weak and incapable of obeying God the way I wanted.

Then, making sure no one was looking, I got down on my knees and prayed a very rational prayer using the verses I'd just read.

Father, I place my life completely in Your hands. I surrender everything to You—spirit, soul, and body. I confess and renounce all sin. [A bunch of sin came to mind and I gladly confessed it all.] If there is any other sin of which I am currently ignorant, bring it to the light. I commit to You now that I will repent of any other sin You show me in the future. I want to be clean, so clean me out.

Your Word says, "If anyone is thirsty, let him come to me and drink." Well, Lord, I am thirsty for You, so keep Your word.

You say, "Do not get drunk on wine, but be filled with the Spirit." Father, I can't do this to myself; I am here asking You to fill me.

You say You give the good gift of the Holy Spirit to those who ask, so I'm asking.

Now, Lord Jesus, You are the One who saturates us in the Holy Spirit. Just as a minister lowered me under water the day I was baptized, immerse me now in Your

Holy Spirit. Saturate every cell in my body, every area of my life, every relationship. Your Word says, "Did you receive the Spirit by works of the law or by hearing with faith?" Well, I am not receiving anything by feeling, but by faith. By faith right now I receive the filling of Your Holy Spirit.

Then I worshiped God for some time. When I got up off my knees, there were no bells or whistles. No thunder or lightning. I didn't feel anything unusual. I didn't speak in tongues. But I knew without a doubt, based on the Word of God, that I had been filled with the Holy Spirit.

Over the subsequent weeks, I noticed distinct changes in my life. Much to my surprise, I was deeply convicted of sin. Within weeks I had called more than thirty people to ask their forgiveness for ways I had offended them. While this was a consequence of being filled I had not anticipated, I could understand that when the *Holy* Spirit filled me, He would expose buried unholiness.

I soon began to share my faith with pre-Christians, and many of them prayed to receive Christ. In addition, I noticed a new joy in worship and singing to the Lord. While I still do not have a great voice, I refer to myself as a member of the "joyful-noise club." I now love to raise my voice to God in praise and worship. Perhaps most noticeably, my prayer life has been constantly growing and increasingly relevant ever since.

REFLECTIONS

It's been many years since I first prayed that prayer. Since then I have received fresh infillings thousands of times.

Though there isn't a formula for receiving the fullness of the

Holy Spirit, you can respond to the Person of the Holy Spirit just as I did. The Spirit wants to fill you with the fire of His fresh revelation of God in Christ.

The Welsh revival began on September 28, 1904, when the young Evan Roberts taught a congregation to pray, "Holy Spirit, fill me now for Jesus Christ's sake." Before the evening was over, God's Spirit swept through that building. Soon revival spread across the British Isles and far beyond. "Holy Spirit, fill me now for Jesus Christ's sake" is not a formula either, but it sure helped hungry people connect with God.

Remember, we are not talking about seeking experience for the sake of a thrill. We are talking about encountering the living God for the sake of empowered, changed lives.

$$\text{\small ≀ ≀ ≀}$$

What about you? Are you hungry for more of God? Is something stirring in you to encounter the fullness of the Holy Spirit that will manifest God's presence right down the middle of your life? In the next chapter we will learn how to take some initial steps toward developing this more intimate relationship with the Holy Spirit.

CHAPTER FOUR

FILLED WITH FIRE

*Oh, why will they split hairs? Why don't they see that
this is just the one thing that they themselves need?
They are good teachers, they are wonderful teachers,
and I am so glad to have them here, but why will they
not see that the baptism with the Holy Ghost is just
the one touch that they themselves need?*
D. L. MOODY[1]

The god who answers by fire—he is God.
THE BIBLE[2]

Yesterday I met with two men who were hungry for God. They had
driven all the way from North Carolina to Atlanta just to talk
with me about being filled with the Holy Spirit.

When one called to make the appointment, I recognized in him
an unusually deep and sincere passion for God. When I tried to
schedule my usual forty-five-minute meeting, he said, "Oh no, that's
not nearly enough time; could we have three hours with you?" He
added, "When we heard you preach on the Holy Spirit, we recognized that you had something we wanted."

They came the night before, stayed at a hotel, and had a quiet,
relaxed morning, so they would be refreshed when we met. They

wanted to be alert so they could receive as much benefit from our meeting as possible.

And receive they did! By the end of our meeting, they had both been saturated by the Holy Spirit. There was no doubt about it; God had met them. It was refreshing to have a front-row seat as God met the deepest longings of these two brothers' souls.

The irony is that the morning we were to meet I had quietly lamented, *Lord, why in the world did I ever schedule this appointment when I have this book to finish? Three hours? Just think how much writing I could get done in three hours.* Yet later as I sat in my office, stimulated by their spiritual passion and doing my best to answer their questions faithfully and biblically, I reflected, I'm sorry, Lord. These are the guys for whom I'm writing this book. What a knucklehead I was!

I heard the Holy Spirit say, *Serve these brothers. They are the hungry ones. As you guide them to be filled with the Holy Spirit, you will be better equipped to help others.*

As my North Carolina friends were led to a fresh encounter with God, let me share with you the steps they took.

TALKING IT OVER

They were full of questions about the Holy Spirit. Though I introduced the biblical rationale for the filling of the Holy Spirit in the last chapter, I'd like to share with you several of the principles we talked about. This matter of developing a vibrant relationship with the Holy Spirit is too important to skim over. While God will manifest Himself uniquely to each of us, there are certain principles from which we can all benefit.

Relating to the Holy Spirit

We need to understand that, whether we consciously acknowledge it or not, we are in relationship with the Holy Spirit. Because the Spirit is a gentleman and does not force Himself on us but leaves the yielding of our wills to us, we are frequently abusive to Him. As we have seen, the Bible mentions several ways we can mistreat the Holy Spirit; we can resist Him, insult Him, lie to His face, spit on Him in blasphemy, make Him sad, and quench His flaming presence.[3] Let's look in more detail at two of the ways we can be abusive to the Holy Spirit.

First, Ephesians 4:30 tells us, "Do not grieve the Holy Spirit of God." To "grieve" means to cause Him sorrow, to offend Him, or to hurt His feelings. As we read the context of this verse, we discover that it is our sins that cause the sorrow. The sins of extreme anger, lying, deceit, bitterness, unforgiveness, and sharp, cutting words are specifically mentioned. We can envision the Person of the Holy Spirit working inside us attempting to restrain all our harsh, stubborn, selfish behavior. He is a force to be reckoned with, but when we fail to obey, we cause Him pain.

Second, we can throw a wet blanket on Him and stifle His positive influence. First Thessalonians 5:19 says "Quench not the Spirit" (KJV), or in the New International Version, "Do not put out the Spirit's fire." The context for this verse lists activities the Holy Spirit loves to mobilize, including unceasing prayer, continual rejoicing, and giving thanks to God in all circumstances. Here Paul pictures the Holy Spirit as a Choirmaster who leads our souls in worship and an indwelling Intercessor who stirs up prayer relevant for every situation. Our problem is that we tend to squelch Him and resist His initiative.

In summary, we grieve the Holy Spirit when we actively do what He is telling us *not* to do. On the other hand, we *quench* the Holy Spirit when we refuse to do what He is telling us to do. They are both sins against the indwelling Person of the Holy Spirit. The one is an active sin; the other is passive. The good news is that there is a better way.

In order to eliminate our maltreatment of the Holy Spirit, we want to give Him free rein. No more stepping on His toes. No more pushing Him off into a corner and barging ahead with our decisions regardless of His input. From now on, we want to give Him preference so that He can express God's rule over every area of our lives and on every one of our relationships. Our money, morals, marriage, sex life, thought life, private life, hobbies, spare time, career—you name it, and God the Holy Spirit will transform it. He gains that position of supremacy by filling us to overflowing with His presence.

Permission to Seek

It is also critical to understand that we have God's permission both to ask for the Holy Spirit and to receive more of His influence in our lives. Some theological streams teach that when you become a follower of Christ you receive all of the Holy Spirit's influence you will ever get. Yet Jesus told His followers, "If you then, though you are evil, know how to give good gifts to your children, how much more will your Father in heaven give the Holy Spirit to those who ask him!"[4] Obviously it is not wrong to ask God for more or Jesus would not have told us to do so.

On another occasion, Jesus stood up at a feast and declared, "If anyone is thirsty, let him come to me and drink. Whoever believes in me, as the Scripture has said, streams of living water will flow from within him." The gospel writer adds, "By this he meant the Spirit."[5] Here again we see Jesus wanting us to desire the Holy Spirit's presence.

After His resurrection, Jesus told His disciples, "Receive the Holy Spirit." To reinforce the significance of reception, He even breathed on them with a demonstrative exhale.[6] When Paul told the Christians in Ephesus, "Be filled with the Spirit,"[7] he was underscoring that though they already had the Spirit's influence because they were already believers, they were not necessarily filled with the Spirit.

Our pursuit of the Holy Spirit begins with a desire born deep in our bellies to know God better and better. The Bible is full of people who unashamedly longed to be filled with more of God. King David and the apostle Paul are just two examples.

- King David cried, "O God, you are my God, earnestly I seek you; my soul thirsts for you, my body longs for you, in a dry and weary land where there is no water."[8]
- The apostle Paul begged, "I want to know Christ and the power of his resurrection and the fellowship of sharing in his sufferings, becoming like him in his death. . . . Forgetting what is behind and straining toward what is ahead, I press on toward the goal to win the prize for which God has called me heavenward in Christ Jesus."[9]
- Paul not only cried out for a fuller revelation of God in his own life, but he also begged for the same for all of God's people: "I keep asking that the God of our Lord Jesus Christ, the glorious Father, may give you the Spirit of wisdom and revelation, so that you may know him better."[10]

No one would suggest that the apostle Paul was unsaved. What we find in these verses is deep hunger for more of God in Christ. The answer for such hunger is the fullness of the Holy Spirit. Remember, the Spirit's ministry is to make Christ known to us.

A. W. Tozer wisely said, "No one has ever been filled with the Holy Spirit who didn't first believe he could be filled with the Holy Spirit."[11] For our purposes we could say, *No one has ever received the fire of God who did not first believe he or she could receive fire.* I hope that by now you realize the Bible gives you permission to come boldly to God and receive the fullness of the Holy Spirit by faith.

Faith, Not Effort

We must also understand that while being filled requires faith, it takes essentially no effort on our part. Just as we can't possibly work our way into heaven, we can't possibly work to fill ourselves with the

Holy Spirit. We receive salvation as a gift that we can't earn and don't deserve, and the filling of the Holy Spirit is also a free gift.

Unlike other commands we receive from God, the imperative to "be filled with the Spirit" is not in the active voice; it's in the passive. We are told to "pray in the Spirit" with an active imperative verb—something we are expected to initiate. But when we are told to be filled with the Spirit, the passive voice indicates it is something that must happen to us.

It was at precisely this point that I was left wandering in the wilderness during the early years of my spiritual journey. I was trying hard to obey God and failing miserably. I tried desperately to pray and read the Word, yet it was dry and lifeless. Then a light went on, and I realized that being filled with the Spirit was not something I did to myself but something God did to me.

Fire Assurance

Just as it is vitally important to have the assurance of salvation, it is vitally important to be assured that we are filled with the Holy Spirit. We can't be tentative about something so important. God wants us to be filled and He wants us to know for certain that we are filled. When Christ told His disciples to "receive the Holy Spirit," He used a physical demonstration to reinforce the action. He literally breathed on them.[12] Jesus wanted His disciples to get it.

Both the assurance of salvation and the assurance of being Spirit-saturated are gifts of God to be received by faith. Paul asked the believers in Galatia a rhetorical question: "Did you receive the Spirit by observing the law, or by believing what you heard?"[13] The obvious answer is that we receive the Holy Spirit (and His fullness) by faith. While there does need to be evidence of His filling, we do not base our assurance on the subjectivity of our emotional response but on the objectivity of God's unshakeable promise.

Paul said to the believers in Rome, "I know that when I come to you, I will come in the full measure of the blessing of Christ."[14] This "full measure of the blessing of Christ" is none other than the fullness of the Holy Spirit. There is no way we can experience the full measure of Christ's blessing without being filled with the Spirit. After all, it is the Spirit's ministry to reproduce the blessing of Christ in us. And did you notice the confidence with which Paul spoke? He said, "I *know*." He was speaking with assurance out of the overflow of his own experience. God wants each of us to have that same filled-to-the-brim-with-Him certainty that comes from being conspicuously Spirit-filled.

THE PROMISE OF FIRE

Even after talking over biblical principles, some sincere seekers are still caught by the question, Is the biblical doctrine of being filled with the Holy Spirit true to my theological roots? Do those whom I doctrinally trust share this view?

Let me remind us that virtually every orthodox Christian denomination began with a solid grip on the "promise of the Father." We find thousands of promises in the Bible, but only one of them is called "the promise of the Father." Jesus told His disciples "I am going to send you what my Father has promised; but stay in the city until you have been clothed with power from on high." Again He said, "Do not leave Jerusalem, but wait for the gift my Father promised." And Peter confirmed, "You will receive the gift of the Holy Spirit. The promise is for you and your children and for all who are far off."[15] The promise is none other than the promise of the filling of the Holy Spirit. Nearly every denomination knew this promise by a genuine encounter with God.

- The Methodists started with a solid belief in the filling of the Holy Spirit. The fire of God's revelation touched John Wesley, father of the Methodists. Early in his ministry he said, "I felt my heart strangely warmed." Later he would not ordain a person into the ministry who could not communicate how he had been filled with the Holy Spirit. Wesley knew that only those pastors who had encountered the fullness of the Spirit could lead their people to such an encounter.

- The Presbyterians and those in the Reformed faith believed in the filling of the Holy Spirit. John Calvin referred to the church as "the fellowship of the flaming heart." He even adopted the flaming heart as the symbol of his movement.

- The Lutherans believed in the filling of the Spirit. Martin Luther, father of the Lutheran Church, wrote in his majestic hymn "A Mighty Fortress Is Our God," "The Spirit and the gifts are ours."

- The Baptists looked to Charles Finney, who talked repeatedly of "my baptism in the Holy Ghost." He said, "It seemed to come in waves and waves of liquid love; for I could not express it in any other way. It seemed like the very breath of God."[16] Multiple signs and wonders accompanied his ministry.

- Other fundamentalists and Bible churches look to R. A. Torrey and D. L. Moody, who experienced being filled with the Holy Spirit. Moody talked of his "baptism with the Holy Ghost." In fact, his close friend Torrey gave an extended account of Moody's encounter in the inspiring book *Why God Used D. L. Moody,* in which he extensively noted Moody's reliance on the Spirit's infilling.[17]

It is sad to consider how many great churches and church leaders have lost a grip on the promise of the Father. I am reminded of a newspaper story about a dear retired man in Hollywood, Florida, who purchased a 100,000-dollar U. S. Treasury Bond with his life savings. To be cautious, he took his bond to the post office to make a photocopy. He walked straight to the copy machine, picked up the lid, put down the original, lowered the lid, put in his coin, pressed the button, and watched the copy slide to the tray. He picked up his copy, drove home, and proudly showed it to his wife. "Where's the original?" she asked.

He realized his mistake. In his haste to make the copy, he had forgotten the original. He jumped into his car and raced back only to discover that his original was missing. The article stated he was offering a 20,000-dollar reward for its return.

When it comes to the promise of the Father, too many of us are walking around with a photocopy. We are God's children, and practical access to the Father's entire estate is wrapped up in His promise. Yet in our haste, we have laid it aside.

The following week I read the sequel to the retiree's story: His bond was returned. May God be so kind to each of us that we might rediscover the promise of the Father and have a fresh encounter with Him that results in being filled with His Spirit. It is the actual certified bond that gives us the confidence we need when we want to make such a significant withdrawal.

MY NORTH CAROLINA FRIENDS

After two stimulating hours of biblical, theological discussion, I led my North Carolina buddies into our church sanctuary, where we wouldn't be interrupted. It was time to act on what we believed. I sat on the front row; they chose to kneel. They prayed, and I coached them a bit.

While the actual moment of being filled with the Holy Spirit is quite simple and straightforward, being filled is a revolutionary moment, when deep and far-reaching events occur simultaneously inside us. Therefore, it is important to cover certain checkpoints in the process. Here are the elements I encouraged my friends to include in their prayers.

- Submit yourselves to God. God wants total dominion, so verbally give it to Him. *"Father, I present my body to You as a living sacrifice. I yield my mind, will, and emotions to You. I completely submit all that I am and all that I have to Your authority."*
- Confess and renounce any and all sin. He is, after all, the *Holy* Spirit, and it should come as no surprise that He wants to fill an utterly clean vessel. Give the Holy Spirit permission to point out any sin that hasn't yet been brought to the light. And if any sin surfaces that would require you to make public restitution, either legally or interpersonally, tell God you are willing to do so. *"Father, I confess my sin to You. I confess my pride and my unbelief. I give You the green light to uncover any other sin as well. I renounce that hidden sin. I will make restitution no matter what it would involve. I don't want anything to remain in me that displeases You. Root it out. Bring it to the light."*
- Receive the full forgiveness of Christ. We have found it very helpful to intentionally receive forgiveness so that there are no guilt-handles to hold us back from wholeheartedly receiving the fullness of the Holy Spirit. *"Yes, Father, I receive Your forgiveness. It is written that if we confess our sins You are faithful and just and will forgive us our sins and cleanse us of all unrighteousness.[18] So I am forgiven. I am clean. I am holy. There is now no condemnation."*
- Ask God to take back from the enemy any ground you've given over. This is one of the critical elements that takes place when we are filled with the Holy Spirit, so it is helpful once again to be explicit. We want to break off any bondage to the evil one. Renounce any

specific evil strongholds that have had a chronic negative influence in your life (such as bitterness, pride, fear, immorality, spiritual apathy, witchcraft, and so on). *"Father, in the name of the Lord Jesus Christ, I ask You to take back from the enemy any ground I've given over to him. I want to be free from any alien strongholds as evil influences in my life. I renounce pride, bitterness, and fears. Set me free from these evil bondages. Now I take back that ground from the evil one."*

- Now receive by faith the filling of the Holy Spirit. Hold out your hands as if you are receiving a gift. *"Father, right now I receive the filling of Your Holy Spirit in the name of the Lord Jesus Christ. Just as I was baptized in water, immerse me in the water of Your Spirit. Saturate every cell in my body, every area of my life with Your Spirit. Take control of my life. Take control of my body, mind, will, and emotions. Like a river, flow in and through me. By faith, I receive. I am filled. I welcome the fullness of Your Spirit. Hallelujah! Thank You, Jesus."*

It is good to linger here. Enjoy a time of extended worship. Don't rush—it's too important. Allow the Holy Spirit to open doors to new areas of your life. Listen for His voice. He will speak to you. He may uncover further sin He will want you to confess and receive forgiveness for. Or He may uncover an evil stronghold from which He will want to set you free. This is all part of His filling. Take your time.

He may also want to minister healing to sore areas of your soul. Often He will touch tender places of your life, such as areas of woundedness, hurts, or insecurities. He may dig up areas long forgotten, buried but not inconsequential. For this reason, tears are common when people are initially filled. The Holy Spirit wonderfully and powerfully floods our soul with a gully-washer of the love of

God.[19] "Unbearable waves of liquid love" is how the great revivalist Charles Finney described his own encounter. At times it is overwhelming to experience God's waves of love poured fresh into our soul. Receive it. Enjoy it. (Again, let me remind you; try not to dwell on what is happening to you. Keep your eyes on Christ, not on yourself. Continue to worship Christ. Directing our attention to Jesus Christ is, after all, the ultimate ministry of the Spirit.)

Remember, there are no formulas here; one size does not fit all. You are smack-dab in the middle of a significant transition when the God of the universe is filling you with His precious Holy Spirit. He will show Himself to you in ways unique to your situation and to your personality, and you will respond to Him in ways unique to you. You may be overwhelmed with a tangible manifestation, or you may simply know by faith that God has done what He promised to do.

Now that you have initially been filled with the Spirit, you are able to receive by faith the filling on an ongoing, daily basis. You will find yourself frequently praying to be filled, and as you do you will develop a keen sensitivity to the Holy Spirit. You will want to hear His voice and obey His leading.

EVIDENCE OF FIRE

When someone is filled with the Holy Spirit, you'd better believe there will be evidence. For this reason, I like the expression "conspicuously filled." It might be possible to be a closet Christian, but it is not possible to be secretly Spirit-filled.

As it has traditionally been taught, the doctrine of evidence for the filling of the Holy Spirit is both helpful and harmful. It is helpful to realize that, because being filled with God's Spirit is such a monumental experience, there must be evidence of some sort. The teaching can be harmful, however, when we are incorrectly taught that the evidence must be speaking in tongues or some other particular manifestation. Even Jack Hayford, who is called by *Christianity Today* magazine "the gold standard of modern Pentecostalism," acknowledges that while he believes the gift of tongues is available to all Spirit-filled believers, this point of doctrine cannot be conclusively proven from Scripture.[20] Tongues are indeed a valid gift of the Holy Spirit, and the fact that tongues often accompany being filled with the Spirit should not be minimalized. They are not, however, the solitary evidence of being filled.

The reality of the filling of God's Spirit can be evidenced in thousands of ways. You may not notice changes right away; you may be able to see them only as you look back on your journey. An encounter with God so deep and revolutionary, however, must have some profound effect on our lives.

The evidence that should characterize and dominate everyone who has genuinely been filled with the Holy Spirit and is continually being filled is a radical, all-consuming love for Jesus. You show me someone who has been filled with the Spirit, and I will show you someone who is head-over-heels in love with Jesus—someone who enjoys intimacy with Him and who demonstrates his or her love for Christ in a lifestyle of hard-core obedience.

You do not need to wait for the perfect time to be filled with the Holy Spirit. Now is as good as any. Get alone with God, claim the promises of God's flaming fullness by faith, and watch what God will do. Evidence will follow. Guaranteed.

$$\text{\dh} \quad \text{\dh} \quad \text{\dh}$$

Once we are filled with the Holy Spirit, we will enjoy the intimacy with God for which we long. As we live in vibrant love-relationship with Jesus, our prayer lives will soar. Let's find out how.

CHAPTER FIVE

FIRE IN THE PRAYER CLOSET

The ugly fact is that altar fires are either out or burning very low. The prayer meeting is dead or dying.
LEONARD RAVENHILL[1]

Prayer is rebellion against the status quo.
DR. DAVID WELLS[2]

We have come to a critical breaking point when we admit that we can't pray effectively on our own and that we need to rely on the leadership of the Holy Spirit. This is a line of demarcation. In a sense, it is both a finish line and a starting point.

It is a finish line because we are done with pumping up our own prayers like helium-filled balloons and hoping that when we let go they will somehow reach heaven's shore. We are finished self-generating a love relationship with God, finished shouldering the responsibility to win God's favor, and finished bearing the insecurity of not knowing if we are praying properly, praying powerfully, or praying often enough.

We realize that prayer relegates us to the status of paupers. Street beggars. Bag ladies. Coming to this humble conclusion is one of the most liberating moments in our relationship with Christ. We quit trying to force it. We quit trying to impress Him. We quit trying to fake it.

The finish line is also the starting point. It is where we start to be ourselves and where we let God be God. For perhaps the first moment in our lives, we shift from focusing on what *we* do when we pray to what *God* does when we pray. We start to receive His love so that we can respond to His initiative. We start to pray under the influence of the Spirit, in the power of the Spirit, according to the will of the Spirit. My friend, welcome to the incredible world of prayer on fire! This is where the sparks begin to fly.

HELP IS ON THE WAY

Imagine that the publishers of this book somehow carved a hole in its pages big enough to insert a gold bar. When you bought the book, you thought it felt a little heavy, but you had no idea what you would find. But lo and behold, here it is: a bar of pure gold.

Okay, now you may wake up. There's no bar of gold here! But read carefully the following sentences from the Bible. They're worth more than sixteen ounces of solid gold. Paul etched these words from the rugged trail of his own up-and-down prayer journey. He knew his miserable incompetence in prayer, and he knew equally well the exuberance of the Holy Spirit's help.

> In the same way, the Spirit helps us in our weakness. We do not know what we ought to pray for, but the Spirit himself intercedes for us with groans that words cannot express.[3]

Of all the words Paul could have used to describe our common prayer saga, he chose *weakness*. It is translated from the Greek word *asthenia*, which is the universal, all-encompassing word for human weakness. It is used for conditions ranging from physical, mental, and emotional weakness to financial, marital, social, interpersonal, and spiritual weakness. This single word summarizes the sorry condition of our prayer lives.

Even when we want to pray, "we do not know what we ought to pray for." Knowing that Paul, who went on to become a world-class pray-er, knew the reality of prayer deficiency should convince us that there is hope for all of us. There is hope because there is help. Once we claim our weakness, we are free to claim our help—the One who is living invisibly inside our chest cavity. The Holy Spirit is always ready at a moment's notice to communicate effectively with the Father on our behalf.

When Paul said, "The Spirit helps us," the word *help* is translated from the Greek word *sun-anti-lambanetai*. This rare triple-compound word communicates that God is a powerful, take-charge interventionist.

- *Lambanetai* means "to take firm hold of, grasp, get a grip on, to take or receive a gift, or to gain an advantage." It is used in the context of taking a wife in marriage or overcoming an enemy by use of force.
- *Anti* means "to come to the aid of, to take up another's cause, to serve, to do another's job, to do an act of kindness on behalf of another, or to devote oneself to the practice of assisting someone else."
- *Sun* means "to stand with or to join in endless union with."

Put together, these three Greek words pack an enormous punch. The Holy Spirit stands with us in endless union (*sun*) to come to our aid, devoting Himself to assisting us (*anti*) in taking firm hold of God in prayer (*lambanetai*). That is His job. This word describes what He is uniquely qualified to accomplish on our behalf. What a dramatic contrast between our feeble prayer efforts and the relentless resolve of the praying Holy Spirit!

The Holy Spirit's prayer life is unquestionably superior to our own. He is, after all, the third Person of the Trinity. He has an inside track with the Father. But it doesn't end there. As remarkable as it may seem, this same Spirit, whose prayer life is infinitely superior to our own, does more than simply pray for us. He promises to transform our struggling prayer lives into robust, strategic prayer lives. Read the promise again: "The Spirit helps us in our weakness." This means that the Holy Spirit promises to be our own personal prayer Coach. He promises to take responsibility for our chronically weak prayer lives and build them into something strong, relevant, and effective.

When we say "the Spirit helps us," we are not simply talking about getting help as we would if we purchased a software manual and had to figure it out for ourselves from there. We are talking about a personal Helper, the Person of the Holy Spirit. He knows us intimately, loves us explicitly, and promises to transform us thoroughly. To do that, He begins by transforming our prayer lives. Once He gains control of our prayer lives, He can accomplish anything He wants to through us.

PRAY IN THE SPIRIT

The key element of all successful prayer is the presence and motivation of God the Holy Spirit. Paul identified this principle when he told the Ephesians to "pray in the Spirit."[4] "Praying in the Spirit" is not simply referring to speaking in tongues, as some might suggest. While the gift of speaking in tongues would be included, "praying in the Spirit" refers generally to all prayer motivated by the Holy Spirit.

Please don't misunderstand. Let me remind you that prayer on fire—or praying in the Spirit—is not some higher form of prayer, as if to suggest that we are already enjoying pretty good prayer, but if we want to be superpray-ers, we should try prayer on fire. No. That's not it. Prayer on fire is regular ol' everyday prayer that *God fills with His presence.*

How do you know, then, that you're praying in the Spirit? Just as you received the filling of the Spirit by faith, so now you pray in dependence on the Holy Spirit by faith. You can even explicitly ask for His help: "Holy Spirit, I don't know how to pray about this, so help me. I want my prayers to come from You, not me. . . . " Virtually every day I quote the verse "Pray at all times in the Spirit, with all prayer"[5] and I claim those last three words: "with all prayer." By faith I consciously take hold of *all prayer*—whatever level, style, or dimension of prayer God wants me to have—and I trust the Holy Spirit to pray through me.

Sometimes when you're praying in the Spirit, you'll be keenly aware of Holy Spirit assistance. Remember what happened to my buddy and me back in high school? It became obvious that we weren't praying under our own power or our own strength; the Spirit had taken over. At other times, however, it may not seem as though anything supernatural or extraordinary is happening. At such times, it is important to remain consistent in prayer, continually asking for and expecting to receive Holy Spirit help.

As we pray in the Spirit, here are some elements He brings to our prayers.

We will begin to hear the Spirit's voice when we pray. We see everyday Christians learning to recognize the Holy Spirit's voice many times in the book of Acts. On one occasion, when believers in Antioch were praying together, the Holy Spirit said, "Set apart for me Barnabas and Saul."[6] Obviously these early Christians knew how to discern the voice of the Spirit; God wants to teach each of us Holy Spirit voice recognition as well.[7]

Often the Holy Spirit will bring Scripture to mind that He wants us to use while we are praying. It should come as no surprise that the Spirit of God loves the Word of God. The Scriptures are called the "sword of the Spirit,"[8] a weapon that the Spirit uses with skill. If I find myself praying for long without using Scripture, I ask God to speak to me and give me an appropriate Bible verse to quote. Using Scripture in prayer adds faith and gives common ground for agreement in corporate prayer.

Praying in the Spirit moves our prayers from merely working through a list to *cultivating a love-relationship with Christ.* This is why prayer on fire is the cure for prayer boredom, lukewarmness, or hollow religious activity. When the Holy Spirit is fanning our genuine love for Jesus into a white-hot passion, we no longer pray out of duty; we now pray out of delight. Prayer is the arena where our love for Jesus is cultivated.

When we are praying in the Spirit, *our requests focus on Christ.* Because the Holy Spirit's primary function is to put the spotlight on Jesus, just imagine the effect He has on our prayers once He fills us. He is constantly putting the focus on Jesus.

Just consider a few potential needs for which I might normally pray:

- A daughter's pregnancy to be healthy and normal
- An upcoming trip to Los Angeles to be safe and successful
- A pay raise
- A father-in-law's open-heart surgery
- A son to pass his bar exam

Virtually all prayer fueled by the Holy Spirit has two objectives: (1) The desire for God to make Himself known through Christ, and

(2) the desire for people to turn to Him. So let's consider praying for these common requests in a way that will point toward these twin goals. As I pray for my daughter's safe pregnancy, do I simply want her physical well-being, or do I want Christ to be revealed to her in a way that will draw her closer to Him? When my father-in-law has open-heart surgery, am I simply praying for his health, or am I asking God to make Himself known to my father-in-law and to draw his life into deeper intimacy with Christ? Is the real objective for the pay raise simply to make more money, or is it to raise the name of Christ in the workplace and extend the kingdom of God? When our prayers have these two underlying motivations, we can be sure we are praying with Spirit-fueled motives.

Once we begin to pray in the Spirit, all sorts of other Holy Spirit activity is generated in our lives. In one way or another, everything the Holy Spirit accomplishes in us is linked to praying in the Spirit.

- We are able to *hear the Spirit.* To each of the seven churches addressed in the book of the Revelation, God said, "He who has an ear, let him hear what the Spirit says to the churches."[9]
- We are able to be *"led by the Spirit."*[10] When we hear the Spirit's voice in prayer, we can follow His lead.
- We can *be controlled by the Spirit.*[11] Once the Holy Spirit fills every area of our lives, we are able to enjoy the benefits of yielding to the authority of God.
- We can *overcome stubborn sin habits by the Spirit.*[12] Even in those areas of our lives where we have known nothing but moral failure, we can now gain permanent victory.
- We can *share the message of salvation* with power and effect by the Spirit.[13]

We're experiencing prayer on fire when we learn to pray in the Spirit. This leads us to ask, "does prayer bring fire or does fire bring prayer?" That question is like the old riddle, "Which came first, the chicken or the egg?"

WHICH COMES FIRST?

The chicken and egg question is easy. I always assumed it was the chicken, because God doesn't lay eggs. The tougher question is, Which comes first, the prayer or the fire? That is, do we first pray for the Holy Spirit to manifest the presence of God or do we pray because the Holy Spirit has *already* manifested the presence of God? This question is critical not simply because it is intellectually stimulating but because it has practical value. The answer to this question will help us pull together some loose ends.

As I said up front, prayer is what we do and fire is what God does. Prayer on fire is what happens when what we do and what God does slam together. Because none of us naturally seek God, our very desire to seek God is His work in us. Therefore, when we desire to be filled with the Holy Spirit, it is because the Holy Spirit is already at work. When we receive the fullness of the Holy Spirit, we are filled with the Spirit of prayer. We have an increasing love for Jesus and desire to spend extended time with Him. The more time we spend in His presence, the more we want of Him, and the more we pray for fire. Rather than this being a vicious circle, it's a glorious circle. For this reason, the Bible says that we go from strength to strength, from fullness to fullness, from glory to glory.[14]

So, from our perspective, prayer goes first. We cry out to God and God answers by sending the fire of His manifest presence. From God's perspective, He was seeking us even before we prayed. Once He fills us, then we experience the reality of His Spirit working in and through our prayers. Therefore, while in a sense the answer is *all of the above*—at times we pray for the fire of God's tangibly revealed presence and at times His manifest presence draws us to deeper prayer—the emphasis should increasingly shift from what we do in prayer to what God is doing in our prayers. A key to making this shift is praying with cupped hands.

CUPPED HANDS

Several years ago while I was praying, the Holy Spirit said to me, *Cup your hands.* When I questioned what He meant by this, it was as if He said, *When you pray, I want you to hold your hands out in front of you with your palms up, as if you are receiving something from Me—because you are!*

So I immediately began to cup my hands in prayer. At first it felt odd, but I must admit, it made such a difference in my faith and in my perspective. It didn't take long, however, to get tired of cupping my hands. The Holy Spirit didn't let up. *Cup your hands,* He'd say.

I'd argue with Him. "But I don't feel like cupping my hands."

Cup your hands.

"Why do I always need to cup my hands?"

Are you praying in order to receive? He'd ask.

"Yes, Lord."

Then cup your hands.

At this moment the light went on. The Holy Spirit put the pattern of ongoing receiving into my life, and since then I have logged tens of thousands of specific answers to prayer.

That day I recognized the revolutionary principle that governed Jesus' life. He said that He could "do only what he sees his Father doing."[15] When Jesus came to the end of His life, He said to His Father, "I have brought you glory on earth by completing the work you gave me to do."[16] I suddenly realized that Jesus lived by the principle of cupped hands. He constantly received from God in prayer so that as He went about His daily life, He walked into the answers to His prayers. On one occasion He spent the entire night in prayer and then, first thing in the morning, called His disciples one by one.[17] Could it be that He was up all night asking the Father whom He should call? The gospel writer seems to imply a direct connection between Jesus' night in prayer and the selection process for His closest disciples. Jesus is seen here as the receiver; His Father was the initiator.

We are to live in a similar position of perpetual receiving. Our prayer lives are the post office where God's communication is delivered as the Holy Spirit initiates and activates every aspect of our prayers.

- Our worship of God starts with God. God is self-revealing; we can worship Him only when He chooses to reveal Himself to us.
- Repentance and confession of sin also start with God. Only in light of the fresh revelation of God's holiness— His impeccable moral character—can we properly see our shortcomings and openly confess our sin.
- True intercession and petition-prayer starts with God as well. As we have seen, we don't know what we are to pray for, but the Holy Spirit speaks to us and prompts us how to pray.
- Thanksgiving is the one aspect of prayer that seems as though it might begin with us. However, even our gratitude is our response to God's initial goodness to us.

These are just some of the works the Holy Spirit does to assist our prayer lives. I certainly can't give you a formula for what He will do in you. Let's remember, the Holy Spirit is not a program but a Person. We want to learn to listen to the Spirit and let Him gain control of our prayer lives. We have access to more—more grace, more power, more passion, more of God's love, more of His presence. It's ours for the taking. Let's cup our hands and continually receive from God's limitless resources.

$$\delta \quad \delta \quad \delta$$

When the Holy Spirit takes hold of our prayer lives, He begins to stir both prayer and the passion for prayer in us in ways we never imagined. A whole new world awaits us. But first we must get our prayer lives out of the aquarium.

CHAPTER SIX

OUT OF THE BOX

I lack the fervency, vitality, life in prayer which I long for.
I know that many consider it fanaticism when they hear
anything which does not conform to the conventional,
sleep-inducing eulogies so often rising from Laodicean lips;
but I know too that these same people can tolerate sin in their
lives without so much as tilting one hair of their eyebrows.
Cold prayers, like cold suitors, are seldom effective.
JIM ELLIOT[1]

The power given is not a gift from the Holy Spirit. He,
Himself, is the power. Today He is as truly available and
as mighty in power as He was on the day of Pentecost.
HUDSON TAYLOR[2]

I don't mind admitting to you that one of my favorite movies is Disney's *Finding Nemo.* I like it for two reasons: My three-year-old grandson likes it—at this stage, anything he likes, I like—and I admire Nemo's spirit. He knows there is more to life than what he is experiencing inside the box.

All the other fish in the aquarium have lost the longing for their ocean home and resigned themselves to their miserable little tank. But not Nemo. Seeing Nemo's face every time he bumps his little nose into the plate-glass aquarium walls is hilarious. The shock. The bewilderment. The crushing disappointment. Nemo refuses to submit to the confines of an aquarium because he knows he was born for the ocean. His tenacity leads to his own courageous journey back to the ocean; his friends follow his lead and find their way back as well.

Too many of us have settled for aquarium-bound prayer lives. We keep swimming in circles and bumping our noses into invisible barriers. We have forgotten that there is so much more out there. When we refuse to be stuck in a little tank, however, we can enter into the ocean of God's Spirit.

BOXED IN NATURALISM

I want to introduce you to a box that keeps us swimming in circles. For those of us who live in the Western world, it is the most common box of all. We bump into it everywhere we turn. It appears in every public-school classroom, government office, and justice building. In some ways this box is huge: It contains the universe, international affairs, governments, education, science, sociology, philosophy, and psychology. In other ways, this box is small: It does not contain prayer, worship, awe, contrition, repentance, the supernatural, or God.

The box I am referring to is *naturalism*. This philosophy says that all of life is governed by natural causes. Immanuel Kant, Søren Kierkegaard, Charles Darwin, Karl Marx, Albert Camus, Jean-Paul Sartre, and a host of other systems thinkers taught the box.

Whether we like it or not, those of us who were born in the Western world grew up inside this box. We've been taught that what is real can be proven in a test tube; anything beyond that cannot be trusted. Honest, objective, thinking people must logically be religious agnostics who believe, *"We can't be sure whether or not God exists; but if He does exist, He's irrelevant to daily life.*" The rude reality of this box is that it has a lid on it. Naturalism refuses to consider, honestly and objectively, the invisible, unseen spiritual realities around us.

Even though we as Bible-believing Christians might hate to admit it, we have in many ways placed God inside the box. If the facts were known, many of us are theoretical supernaturalists, but in reality we are practicing naturalists. We have distanced ourselves from the supernatural manifestations of God, believing them to be philosophically impossible. And if our worldview is naturalistic, it is reasonable to assume that our prayer lives have been stunted inside the box.

Don't misunderstand; we can still pray inside the box. That is no problem. People do it all the time. Prayer in the box, however, is bland, harmless, anemic, routine, earthbound, faithless, heartless, hopeless, and—worst of all—fireless. While there are all kinds of prayers inside the box, there is no fire. As you would expect, fire goes out in the box—it is not possible for God to manifest Himself in any way. That would not be tolerated.

It is time for us to take the lid off and climb out of the box. As Christians, we are by definition philosophical supernaturalists, so we need to repent of allowing naturalism to crush our faith and hinder what we believe God can do. We are followers of the One who physically rose from the dead. Like nothing else in history, the single act of Christ's resurrection permanently blows the lid off the box. In light of the Resurrection, we are all invited to step out of the box and into the supernatural. The Bible even warns us against "having a form of godliness but denying its power."[3] We have quenched the Spirit's fire and lived without the fresh breath of God's reviving presence for far too long. Our worldview tells us that God is active and relevant to our daily lives; now let's live like it. Let's pray like it.

BOXED IN OUR THEOLOGY

Sometimes even our theology keeps us boxed in. Cessationism theology says that certain gifts of the Holy Spirit have ceased. Adherents of this view teach that God worked in certain ways in former dispensations but that He does not work that way anymore.

Dr. Jack Deere is a former Dallas Theological Seminary professor who taught that the manifestation gifts had ceased. "I was the most unlikely candidate in the world for the joke God was about to play on me,"[4] he says. The joke he is referring to is that he was unexpectedly filled with the Holy Spirit and experienced a fresh encounter with God. His thoughtful book *Surprised by the Power of the Spirit* tells how he climbed out of the box, taking his biblical theology and his prayer life with him.

Dr. J. Vernon McGee is another brother in Christ who had taught that healing, along with other manifestations, had ceased in the first century. His preaching was broadcast on more than four hundred radio stations and translated into more than one hundred languages. Then he was diagnosed with terminal cancer. After radical surgery, doctors gave him only six months to live. People all over the world prayed for his healing, and—though it contradicted McGee's worldview—God chose to heal him and extended his life twenty-three years![5] God really does have a sense of humor, doesn't He? After God healed his terminal cancer, McGee was glad to change his doctrinal views of healing, at least modestly.

Christian theology doesn't do well in a box. It is no accident that the only two continents on the planet where church growth is not taking place—North America and Europe—are both stuck in the box. In other cultures, a supernaturalist worldview dominates, and the church is thriving. Hundreds of stories are surfacing of Muslim people who are coming to faith in Jesus Christ because of God's supernatural intervention. God the Father is speaking to them in visions and dreams about His Son Jesus Christ and the true book of God, the Bible. Why? Although Muslims are strict in some ways, their worldview allows for supernatural revelatory gifts.

God's manifestation of Himself through the gifts of prophecy, healings, words of knowledge, miracles, tongues, and interpretation of tongues are all outside the box. It may be a stretch for some of us to embrace God's supernatural manifestations and giftings, but sometimes climbing out of a box requires stretching.

The great Bible scholar and preacher at Westminster Chapel of London, Dr. Martyn Lloyd-Jones, said regarding the revelatory manifestation gifts, "The Bible was not given to replace direct revelation; it was given to correct abuses."[6] Because I love the Bible and honor its authority over all of life, this perspective enables me to be open to current revelation, knowing that it is all subject to the ultimate authority of God's inerrant Word.

BOXED IN OUR FEAR OF COUNTERFEITS

Another box that can keep us away from what God wants to do in our lives is our disgust for misplaced spiritual zeal and false manifestations. We have seen so much smoke without fire that we are in danger of rejecting the idea of fire altogether. And there are valid reasons for concern. Any discerning person these days should be objective as he or she evaluates the increasingly complex Christian landscape.

Let me remind you that the existence of phony fire does not disprove the existence of true fire. If anything, the presence of a counterfeit normally verifies that there *is* an original. I have in the jewelry box on my dresser a knockoff Rolex watch someone gave me. Such watches are sold in every major city around the world. The reason the knockoff exists, however, is because somewhere there is a genuine.

There are countless examples of false fire, and we could never do justice to them all. In simple terms, though, there are two sources of false fire or counterfeit manifestations of God: They are of either demonic or human origin.

Demonic Counterfeits

Make no mistake; Satan can counterfeit the miracles of God. We see it in the Old Testament when Pharaoh's magicians copied God's miracles by utilizing demonic powers.[7] In the New Testament, we encounter slippery Simon who tried to buy Peter's miracle-working powers.[8] Even the coming Antichrist will perform impressive signs and wonders.[9] In our own day there are demonic counterfeit miracles as well.

I had taken a group of students from my church to Boston's Tremont Temple for a Barry McGuire concert. I love Barry. His heart and voice are refreshing. But this was not his night. He struggled every inch of the way through the first set of songs. After forty-five minutes he tried to lead in prayer. From the balcony someone cut loose with a loud, shrieking voice in an unknown language. The already-strained atmosphere got worse. I knew Barry well enough to realize he was praying silently and asking God for direction. *What's he going to do?* I wondered. *Lord, help him!* I prayed.

Barry put his mouth near the microphone, pressed his tongue between his lips, and gave one of the best Bronx cheers I've ever heard. "Get that thing out of here," he directed. "That is not of God and doesn't belong in here." Barry sang another song and ended the concert unusually early. My group filed out of the concert hall in awkward silence and quietly boarded the bus. *How many parents will call me about this one?* I wondered.

Ten minutes into our ride home, one of the guys came and sat down next to me. "Was that what I think it was?" he soberly asked.

"What do you think it was?" I responded.

"A demonic tongue?"

I nodded in affirmation. After another pensive minute, he inquired, "Would you pray with me? I need to get right with God. I haven't been living for God. But that voice was so creepy I want to make sure my life is submitted firmly to Christ. After what I heard tonight, I sure don't want to have anything to do with the devil."

That shrieking voice is only one example of counterfeit fire. God certainly gives the gift of tongues to people today, enabling them miraculously to speak in languages they never learned.[10] And because there is a genuine, there is also a counterfeit. When the devil inspires counterfeits, God graciously gives discernment to His people. Christ will even use the sicko, knockoff, false fire of demonic miracles to work for His honor and glory if we let Him.

Human Counterfeits

There are also examples of human efforts to impersonate the activity of God. Sometimes we try to get our mitts on God's holy stuff.

I can remember sitting offstage awaiting my PTL Club television interview about a book I had recently written. Jim and Tammy Faye Bakker were chatting onstage about how the past month's statistics showed that their TV show had registered more professions of faith in Christ than Billy Graham's, Robert Schuller's, Jimmy Swaggart's, Pat Robertson's, or anyone else's. Tammy Faye gloated, "Jim, that means God is using you more than anyone else in the world." Jim just sat there with his sheepish grin and nodded in agreement. Something smelled wrong. I was not surprised months later when their ministry collapsed and their marriage ended with Jim behind bars.[11] What happened?

I believe God was genuinely using the Bakkers, but they touched the fire. In the past several years, Jim has repented and even through his prison sentence has genuinely encountered God's manifest presence.

Jim and Tammy Faye are not the only ones to cross the invisible line of demarcation separating the holy and the common. The name the Bible uses for this irreverent gesture is "unauthorized fire."[12] Today it happens when people casually touch God's flaming presence or attempt to manipulate His activity for personal gain.

Be assured that nothing draws God's ire like false fire. I know it rhymes, but it's true nonetheless. The fire of God's presence is much too precious for Him to sit back and let us manhandle it. Anyone with a cavalier attitude toward God's special stuff is in for a rude awakening. Like cheap perfume that makes a boyfriend want to push away, faking God's presence is a stench in His nostrils. False fire normally makes Him want to push away, and at times it even makes His blood boil.

It is unfortunate that some of us may have been introduced to the counterfeit first, but we shouldn't allow the false to immunize us against the genuine. The answer to false fire—whether of demonic or human origin—is not the rejection of the manifestations of God's presence, but the embracing of holy fire. When the genuine fire is generated when the Holy Spirit ignites our hearts, we no longer have any need to mess with—or fear—the counterfeits.

So, what would it look like to take our faith, the Bible, and our prayer lives out of the box? That's an exciting question.

LIVING OUTSIDE THE BOX

Jesus flattened every box. He walked on water, cast out demons, raised twelve-year-olds from the dead, and met with Elijah and Moses on a shining mountain. He said, "The Son can do nothing by himself; he can do only what he sees his Father doing."[13] Jesus saw into the invisible world and recognized the works and intentions of God. He joyfully joined the Father in His activities.

As followers of Jesus, out-of-the-box living is for us too. He wants us to join Him in doing His Father's work. After all, He said, "Anyone who has faith in me will do what I have been doing. He will do even greater things than these, because I am going to the Father."[14] Jesus hands us the key to out-of-the-box living: faith. Faith is the element that moves us from being naturalists to being supernaturalists. And God loves faith. The Bible says, "Without faith it is impossible to please God."[15] Or to say it another way, If we want to make God really happy, we want to step into His supernatural activity in our lives.

What will it look like for you to exercise faith that God is supernaturally at work? We've already seen two ways: Receive the filling of the Holy Spirit and allow Him to mentor us in prayer. Now we are ready to experience life outside the box. We are ready to do what Jesus did: See into the invisible world, recognize the works and intentions of God, and then joyfully join the Father in His activities.

Stepping out of the box will probably look different for me than it will for you. God has His own way of stretching each of us and moving us to faith. Just think of the many ways He asked people in the Bible to recognize and join Him:

- He asked Abraham to sacrifice his only son.
- He asked Moses to lead God's people out of Egypt.
- He asked Daniel to stand in front of hungry lions.
- He asked Jonah to go to Nineveh.
- He asked Mary to bear an "illegitimate" child, and
- He asked Joseph to raise Him.
- He asked Peter to walk on water.
- He asked a man with a deformed hand to stretch it out, something the man had never done before.

The list could go on and on, but allow me to make a few observations. First, notice that every time God invited His people to join Him outside the box, He took the initiative. He clearly communicated the assignment to His people, and they rose to the challenge.

This teaches us the important lesson that true faith is a response to God's invitation. False faith, on the other hand, is often generated when we act on our own, trying to initiate a venue for God's miraculous power to be displayed. Not a good idea. We don't need to make God look better or manufacture our own miracles. He creates the God-moments, and we step into them.

Second, notice that God's invitations required His people to take a step of faith. For God's people to obey, they needed to trust their lives to His supernatural intervention. As we have said, the only way to make God truly happy is to take a faith step in obedience.

Third, notice the reluctance many of these people displayed. Many of them seriously struggled and at least one of them—Jonah even tried to run away. We need to understand that God knows how we're wired. He knows we struggle to exercise faith, particularly those of us raised in the mindset of naturalism. Henry Blackaby calls this inner struggle "the crisis of belief," where we decide whether to stay put or to go with God.[16]

Finally, each of these seekers encountered the manifest presence of God once they stepped out. Abraham found the ram in the thicket after he built the altar. David won a giant victory over Goliath after he stepped onto the battlefield. Daniel got a front-row seat to watch God close the mouths of lions after he defied a royal decree in order to pray. And the list goes on.

The good news is that Jesus is very good at getting God's people to become true supernaturalists. After all, He isn't called the "author and finisher of our faith"[17] for nothing!

PRAYING OUTSIDE THE BOX

The easiest way to determine if your faith is in the box is to evaluate your prayer life objectively. Simply ask yourself, When I pray, am I expecting God to penetrate my world? Or even more far-reaching, What ministry initiative am I involved in that is doomed to failure unless God intervenes? How much fire—or how much of God's manifest presence—am I seeing in answer to prayer?

When we learn to exercise faith while praying, our prayers open the door and invite God's supernatural activity into our world. Jesus said that with true faith we can tell a mountain to be cast into the ocean and it will happen. "Therefore, I tell you," He added, "whatever you ask for in prayer, believe that you have received it, and it will be yours."[18] At one point He was unable to perform miracles because of the people's unbelief,[19] and on another occasion His faith Geiger counter started beeping relentlessly because He recognized faith in one person that exceeded that of anyone else in all Israel.[20] Faith floods the atmosphere when God is ready to manifest His presence; unbelief, on the other hand, shuts down the atmosphere. We certainly want to be among those who cultivate a climate of faith.

Allow me to tell two stories that illustrate prayers of faith. During graduate school, I was a youth pastor of an awesome group of forty students just north of Boston. These students loved Jesus and had encountered His radical presence. They wanted to share Him with their entire student body. They prayed and asked God for a method of communicating His love, and someone suggested giving a small New Testament to every student. While it would have been illegal to pass them out formally, it was permissible to give to those who asked. So they decided to carry a New Testament conspicuously on top of their other books. When anyone would ask what it was, they would say, "It's the New Testament. Here, take it; it's free."

There was just one problem. There were a thousand students in the high school, and we didn't have any Bibles. We prayed and asked God for Bibles. The next night, a girl in the group called me all excited with the news that her dad had two hundred copies of exactly the Bible we wanted to give away, and that he had donated them to our cause. Praise the Lord!

Two weeks later all those Bibles had been distributed, so we prayed again. Within a week we received a letter from the New York Bible Society. They had published the Bible we were distributing and were so excited over our effort they volunteered to give us the eight hundred copies that remained in their supply—exactly the number we yet needed! You can only imagine how jazzed the students were at this conspicuous answer to specific prayer.

Similarly a youth group in Michigan learned that the heavy-metal rock group KISS was coming to the Glacier Dome in Traverse City to do a concert. They, too, believed that with God anything is possible. They asked God to cancel the concert. As they prayed, they sensed God saying to them, *Okay, I hear you. I will cancel the KISS concert. They will not play as scheduled.*

The students were thrilled. They told their friends that KISS would not play. But as the concert date approached, the Christian students got a bit nervous because it appeared the concert would happen without a hitch. The concert sold out. The band with painted faces and platform shoes stepped onto the stage. The lead guitarist picked up his guitar, brought his arm down over the strings . . . and immediately behind him, twelve thousand dollars worth of electronic equipment blew up. For an hour the crew tried in vain to repair it. The concert was cancelled, and the record shows KISS did not perform. I can assure you that those Christian students tasted the joy and exhilaration of praying outside the box.[21]

DREAM AGAIN

It's time to dream again. It's time to dream of what if. *What if* I climbed out of the box? *What if* I let my faith out of the box? *What if* my prayer life were free of the box? *What if* I began asking God to work, manifesting His presence in tangible ways?

This is a most exciting time for you as you face the prospects of climbing out of the box and setting your faith free. Let me remind you that you do not want to run off on your own and scheme up a miracle. It is all too easy to push a newfound freedom to excess. Faith is not self-induced; it's the gift of God and comes in response to God's Word to us.

Rather than barging ahead, be patient. Sit and wait on the Lord. Learn to hear His voice. Let Him lead you in prayer. He wants to give you very specific prayer assignments, telling you precisely what to pray for. The key to receiving from God is learning to ask for the things that are already on His heart.

God is constantly at work around us, and He will invite you to join Him in His activity. All we need to do is learn to listen to His voice with an inclination to obey. *Faith* believes reality is outside the box. *Obedience* climbs out and joins Him in His activity.

Whether they come from our philosophy or our theology, our boxes are dealt a deathblow as we consistently encounter the manifest presence of God. Like Nemo finding himself out of the aquarium and back in the ocean, we are free to swim in the great big supernatural ocean of God's manifest presence.

ᘐ   ᘐ   ᘐ

Jesus is very good at getting us out of the box. As exhilarating as it is to take our first steps into the supernatural, it quickly becomes overwhelming. The next chapter focuses on a topic few books dare to discuss but which we will all experience when we encounter the fire of God. We might as well face it head on.

CHAPTER SEVEN

ASHES

*Am I ignitable? God deliver me from the dread asbestos
of other things. Saturate me with the oil of your Spirit that
I may be aflame. But flame is transient, often short-lived.
Canst thou bear this, my soul—short life? In me there dwells
the Spirit of the Great Short-Lived whose zeal for God's house
consumed him. And he has promised baptism with the Spirit
and with the Fire. Make me thy fuel, Flame of God.*
JIM ELLIOT[1]

*Let me burn out for God. After all, whatever
God may appoint, prayer is the greatest thing.
Oh that I might be a man of prayer!*
HENRY MARTYN[2]

See, the LORD is coming with fire.
THE PROPHET ISAIAH[3]

When we climb out of the box and throw open wide the door to
God's supernatural activity, wonderful things start to happen.
We start praying for things we never before dreamed of bringing to
God. We see God step into areas of life that had previously seemed
God-forsaken.

We begin to see dramatic answers to specific prayers. Miracles follow: healings and financial provision. You find your misplaced car keys. It is exhilarating and legitimate. But as wonderful as it is, this is not the whole story. Being filled with the fire of the Spirit and enjoying the reality of prayer on fire brings another result that is equally as important as the others; it's just not nearly as much fun.

I'm referring to *ashes*. As I sit in my study writing these words, I am surrounded by hundreds of books on prayer and the work of the Holy Spirit. I have read them all, but none of them told me about ashes. That I had to learn on my own.

Ashes are what happen inside our souls when God shows up in force, and we see Him for who He is. Ashes are, after all, a normal consequence of fire, are they not?

DAKA ASHES

When God manifests His presence, we encounter a *holy* God. And it's quickly obvious that we *aren't* holy. We see our sin for what it is and experience deep conviction. The fire of God's presence touches us, and we are left with the ashes of a contrite spirit.

The Old Testament Hebrew word for this brokenness of spirit is *daka*.

- Isaiah was moved to *daka* brokenness when the white-hot coal of God's holiness was pressed to his sin-dripping lips.[4]
- After Jesus supernaturally enabled him to catch a boatload of fish, Peter was moved to *daka* brokenness and cried, "Go away from me, Lord; I am a sinful man!"[5]
- The early church was moved to contrite hearts when every head caught on fire the day the Spirit rained down.[6]

- Even when the beloved disciple John laid eyes on the
  risen, ascended, and exalted Jesus, he fell at his Lord's
  feet like a dead man.[7]

We don't create the ash of a contrite spirit in ourselves; God does. I was first introduced to this work of God at a Prayer Summit. Prayer Summits are the brainchild of Christian leader Joe Aldrich, who was asking, "What would it take to attract and sustain the manifest presence of God in a geographical area?" While every Prayer Summit is distinct, they all begin by calling participants to lay aside personal agendas and simply worship the exalted Christ. More than a thousand Summits have now been facilitated worldwide, and in virtually all settings, the same thing happens as people seek God in this way: God finds them.

And when He does, their hearts are exposed. Conviction sets in. At my first Pastors' Prayer Summit, I couldn't believe my eyes as I saw a 250-pound, hard-driving, fast-talking pastor run to the center of the prayer circle, screaming out in agony over the conviction of sin, and melting into a puddle on the floor, begging for God's mercy.

To give people an outlet to express their heartfelt sorrow over sin, the Prayer Summits have initiated the Chair. It is placed in the center of the prayer circle. Participants may voluntarily sit or kneel at the Chair and publicly, audibly confess their sins to God.

The unburdening always begins as confession of sins to God. Stuff that has been buried for years comes into the light. Over the years, I've heard Christian leaders confess it all: adultery, pornography, bestiality, extortion, theft—even murder.

Quite often the confession shifts from confession to God to confession to each other. I've heard Baptist pastors acknowledge with tears to charismatic pastors, "I've told my people not to associate with your people." And I've heard charismatic pastors confess to mainline leaders, "I've called you names: 'God's frozen chosen,' 'the dead in Christ.' I have treated you with harsh arrogance. Please forgive me."

When we began to observe the depth of conviction, we coined the phrase *God's rotisserie.*

GOD'S ROTISSERIE

I affectionately use *God's rotisserie* to describe the wonderful process the Holy Spirit uses to bring hidden sin to the surface of our conscience and lead us in repentance. It is as if the Holy Spirit fires up the grill, cranks up the flame, puts us on the skewer, and lets us sizzle for a while until we are done—until we're done hiding, done fighting, done deceiving ourselves, done clinging to control, done with sin.

The initial response to the Holy Spirit's flame is to shrink back, hunker down, dig in deeper, and hide. We are tempted to think, *We've lived with this stuff for years, so we can survive a few more hours.* There is just one problem: God loves us too much to let us get away with it. So what does He do? He turns up the heat. At times we toss and turn all night. But we can't fight the conviction of God forever. Not on God's rotisserie. God has His way of smoking us out.

Listen to what a fourteen-year-old boy wrote about his experience of conviction of sin:

> I do not hesitate to say that those who examined my life would not have seen any extraordinary sin, yet as I looked at myself I saw outrageous sin against God. I was not like the other boys, untruthful, dishonest, swearing and so on. But all of a sudden, I met Moses carrying the law . . . God's ten words . . . and as I read them, they all seemed to join in condemning me in the sight of a thrice-holy Jehovah.

Those words were written in the 1800s by the young Charles Spurgeon.

Good things come out of God's rotisserie. Honesty, humility, transparency, repentance, and obedience are all part of the fruit of godly sorrow over sin. The fire of God's manifest presence will burn out the wood, hay, and stubble of our lives so that only the good stuff remains. Let me introduce you to two of my friends, Molly and John. Both of their hearts were reduced to ashes.

MY FRIEND MOLLY

When Molly called me on the phone, she was desperate. "Fred, I need help," she begged. "I have three choices: I can kill myself, I can have a nervous breakdown, or I can become a Christian."

"Molly, I thought you were a Christian," I said.

"I thought I was too," she replied.

Oh, God. Help me help Molly! I cried out. Immediately a thought popped into my mind: *Ask her if she ever repented.*

"Molly, have you ever repented?" I asked.

"Have I ever what?" Molly asked.

"Have you ever repented? You know, have you ever given Jesus Christ control of your life, turning over the steering wheel of your life to Him?"

"No," she responded. "I have always been afraid of giving God control. Ever since I went through my divorce I've been afraid to trust anyone enough to give them control."

I affirmed Molly's honesty and her willingness to trust me with her thoughts.

Though she was calling from San Francisco and I was living in Miami, we talked on the phone for at least an hour. Yes, she chose option three and became a Christian that day. She prayed with my wife and me on the phone, and she gave God full control of her life.

It was awesome! She actually got on a plane the next day, flew to Miami, and was baptized in our church that next evening. As painful as it was at the time, God's invasive love exposed the sin within Molly and led her in repentance. Her encounter with God's holy presence became a life-giving turning point for her.

MY FRIEND JOHN

John works for CNN. One day while he and I were running, he told me of a remarkable experience he had while flying to Japan to cover the fiftieth anniversary of the atomic bomb drop on Hiroshima. As he was sitting in his airplane seat at 37,000 feet, with no apparent provocation he was overwhelmed with a sense of God's fiery presence. God was revealing Himself to John at a deeply intimate level, and the effect was instant brokenness.

"It was as if I could hear the bones within me breaking," he reported. "I was crying uncontrollably. Even the flight attendant offered me assistance. With tears coursing down my cheeks, I told her unconvincingly that everything couldn't have been better."

What is going on? John had wondered. *I have never felt like this before.* A crushing conviction was going on deep in his soul as he was breaking under the weight of God's grace and goodness. *I have a great wife, a strong marriage, a darling daughter, a great job, and a beautiful home in an upscale neighborhood,* he thought. *Outwardly everything is perfect, but inside I'm unraveling.* When he finally arrived after his twelve-hour flight, he checked into his hotel room, flopped onto the mattress, and found himself weeping all night in the presence of God's glorious holiness.

He explained:

While I was there in Japan, God gave me a powerful picture of what was happening to me in the very story I was covering. You see, after the bomb's devastation, it was universally agreed that plant life would never appear there again. But contrary to predictions, today Hiroshima is brimming with life. Similarly, the ashes of my broken spirit weren't terminal. The Spirit of God is breathing new life into me.

With a big smile, John added, "And now I am clean and I am free."

BEAUTY FROM ASHES

Both John and Molly experienced the invasive, loving work of the Holy Spirit in their lives. Their stories are different, yet both of them were changed. God's intent was not to destroy them. On the contrary, He manifested His presence to them, and in the light of His flame their hearts were exposed. Yes, they were broken, but they weren't harmed, shamed, or discarded. Instead they were cleansed and liberated. They went from *Oh no, God knows everything about me* to *Oh good, God knows everything about me.*

As those who battle lukewarm hearts, we have been afraid of what the invasive, all-consuming fire of God might do; we are afraid it might destroy us. But God loves us so much that when we are broken, He takes a deep breath and blows fresh life into us. Listen to how the prophet Isaiah described this revival principle:

> For this is what the high and lofty One says—
>   he who lives forever, whose name is holy:
>   "I live in a high and holy place,
>   but also with him who is contrite [daka] and
>   lowly in spirit,
>   to revive the spirit of the lowly
>   and to revive the heart of the contrite [daka]."[8]

This level of divine encounter is available to all who dare to embrace the penetration of God's flaming presence.

Though we may think of ashes as useless matter only fit for the trash, God loves them. God is pleased when He spots a worshiper with an ashen spirit who has been incinerated by His all-consuming presence:

> The sacrifices of God are a broken spirit;
> a broken and contrite [daka] heart,
> O God, you will not despise.[9]

True worship comes from exposure to God's volcanic love, standing under the flame of his Word, and gazing at the blinding light of His impeccable character.

God loves ashes because they represent a heart that holds nothing back. An ashen spirit is 100 percent yielded to God. It is no wonder the Bible promises that God will restore beauty in the place of ashes.[10] When nothing hinders God's redemptive purposes in our lives, beauty will come to us.

DAKA AND YOU

What will ashes look like in your life? I don't know. I can't tell you when or how the Holy Spirit will bring you to such an all-consuming fire encounter. But I can assure you that He is an *all*-consuming fire. If you walk in intimacy with Him, sooner or later you will meet Him at a level that will leave you in a pile of ashes. He wants to have your heart to Himself.

One thing I can tell you: You will not need to plan your own spiritual cremation. It is not even appropriate to seek to be consumed. What we are to seek is God's blazing presence. Our focus is to be on Him, not on what happens to us. With wholehearted abandon we are to embrace His activity in our lives and give Him the green light to incinerate anything He wants.

You will likely feel some fear when you think of surrendering to this work of God. After all, God is a Cajun cook. He likes to turn up the heat. None of us want to be held radically accountable or to be exposed. As ironic as it might sound, it is precisely at this point that the fear of intimacy keeps many God-seekers at arm's length from the very God they are seeking. We must confront this unhealthy fear of God that can cause us to shut down just when we are on the verge of a breakthrough in our relationship with Him.

The issue is trust. Will you trust the God who is fire to manifest His consuming presence whenever He chooses? And will you trust yourself to Him? The way you respond to your *daka* moments—whether you shut down, withdrawing off into the corner or you say, "Lord, this is intimidating and even painful, but I trust you anyway"—will determine the authenticity of your prayer life.

I have learned to pray for the rotisserie in my own life and in the lives of those I love. I want the conviction of the Holy Spirit for my family members, my friends, my church family, and myself. The rotisserie is real. It is cleansing, purifying, liberating. It takes off our masks. It breaks off the chains of deception. It delivers us from both our fear of fire and our fear of the Holy Spirit. Most important, it produces in us what the Spirit has been longing for—a yielding of the control of our lives to Christ.

Samuel Logan Brengle, an early leader in the Salvation Army, described his encounter with God's flaming presence: "My soul melted like wax before fire. I sobbed and sobbed. I loathed myself that I had ever sinned against him or doubted him or lived for myself and not for his glory. Every ambition for self was now gone. The pure flame of love burned it like a blazing fire would burn a moth."[11] What

Logan was expressing is *beauty for ashes*. We don't need to shrink from the flame; we want to embrace it. As someone has said, "When we get to heaven, God will not say, "Medium rare, my good and faithful servant!" He will say, "Well done!"

$$\delta \quad \delta \quad \delta$$

The ashen spirit grows out of intimacy with God, and there is nowhere our intimacy with God will be proven more dramatically than in our nuclear family. To be honest, relationships with our spouse or kids can be the most difficult venue in which to see the hand of God. It is time to receive some practical help on how to get those home fires burning, because when the fire of God's manifest presence comes, this is the arena where it is most fulfilling.

CHAPTER EIGHT

KEEPING THE HOME FIRES BURNING

*When the fire is falling, get as near as
you can to the flame.*
ROY FISH[1]

*God can be expected to send revival when those
extraordinary feelings of extraordinary need
provoke an extraordinary sense of His presence.*
RICHARD OWEN ROBERTS[2]

M y three sons and I were ready to tee off at Georgia's Stone Mountain Golf Course when the sounds of honking horns, dozens of runners, and an entourage of pace cars nearly interrupted my backswing.

"Hey, Dad! Look!" my son said, pointing to the nearby road. "The Olympic torch!"

What a sight! A strong, young runner proudly held the flame high above his head as he ran his leg of the flame's journey from Athens to Atlanta for the 1996 Olympic Games. As we stood at attention and observed this, we joined the celebration of bringing the flame. The privilege of carrying the torch and the dignity of the ceremony were impressive.

Several times while standing over putts that day, I thought about the similar, honorable distinction I have of passing the torch of faith to my kids. What a joy and honor to influence my children to love Jesus and to encourage them to respond to the flaming revelation of His presence in our home.

As a young parent I had heard a Christian leader make a statement that marked my life: "If our children do not see dramatic answers to specific prayers, we will lose them to Satan."[3] As I replayed those words in my mind, I thought, *Yikes! Far more than simply wanting to raise good kids, I want to raise champions. I want my children to have a firsthand knowledge of the power of God, not just second- or third-hand information.*

It is our privilege to show our children the flame of God's manifest presence in our homes and to encourage them to embrace the blaze for themselves. We want our kids to recognize clearly that Christ is alive and active today. If they do not experience the conspicuous presence of God firsthand, they will look elsewhere for reality.

It is no coincidence that when the apostle Paul told Turkish Christians to be filled with the Holy Spirit, he then moved into talking with them about seeing God's presence manifested in the home. "Be filled with the Spirit. . . . Wives, submit to your husbands. . . . Husbands, love your wives. . . . Children, obey your parents. . . . Fathers, . . . bring [your children] up in the training and instruction of the Lord."[4] When we are encountering God's manifest presence in our lives, those closest to us will recognize His presence as well.

We will be looking at some practical steps we can take to attract the manifest presence of God to our homes. But first we want to look at one element that can exist undetected in our homes and can do more damage than we would imagine.

ASBESTOS IN THE HOME

There is a fire-extinguishing influence that can subtly make its way into our family life. Like asbestos in our ceiling tiles, it sits there killing us, and often we aren't even aware of the danger. It thrives in children who are raised in second- or third-generation Christian families. It's particularly prevalent in homes of those in professional ministry, such as pastors, missionaries, or Christian leaders. The asbestos we are referring to is the sin of irreverence.

Irreverence is disrespect for the holy things of God. Instead of treating the things of God as special, irreverence brings a casual, even cavalier attitude toward spiritual realities. Its subtle tone of "I know it all—I've heard it a thousand times before" is rooted in pride.

Tragically, irreverence creeps undetected into the homes of godly people. Parents unknowingly pass down a high demand for external compliance. Children learn how to punch all the right buttons, jump through the right hoops, and perform on cue. Going to church, not getting pregnant before marriage, acting polite, and being basically good kids are all part of the script.

There is just one problem: It is all external. Outward compliance simply disguises the absence of true reverence for God. The children experience form without fullness, performance without passion, façade without fire. And we end up with children who honor God with their lips but have hearts far from Him.

One parent who allowed the asbestos of irreverence inside his front door was the Old Testament priest Eli. He was known in the community as a man of God, but he was a lousy parent. The first four chapters of 1 Samuel show us that he had been given the job of maintaining the holy fire in the temple, of all things—a responsibility that should have been met with a heavy dose of sobriety.

The religious system of the day placed his sons in the business with him, and they proceeded to take a casual attitude to new levels. They may have seen Eli, like many who serve in professional ministry, caught up in the monotony of the daily grind, simply going through the motions. And, as the saying goes, what parents tolerate in moderation, children push to excess. Eli's kids were rude to the sincere worshipers and skimmed the cream off the temple offerings. Their irreverence was an insult to God: "This sin of the young men was very great in the LORD's sight, for they were treating the LORD's offering with contempt."[5] The offerings the boys handled with contempt were made with fire, and they mishandled it. Rather than demonstrating a holy trembling, they demonstrated a flippant arrogance.

Not long after their sin was exposed, Philistine armies seized the ark of the covenant and killed Eli's sons. When word of this military defeat reached Eli, he fell off his chair backward, fatally snapping his neck. What a pitiful way to die.

When Eli's pregnant daughter-in-law learned of the triple-whammy, it threw her into such an emotional tailspin that she instantly went into labor and gave birth to a child destined to grow up without a father, uncle, grandfather, or any father figure. More tragically, he would grow up without the presence of God. Appropriately, she named him Ichabod, which means "the glory has departed."[6] The glory of her life had departed when all the men in the family died, but the glory of God's manifest presence had departed as well.

Moral of the story: If you want to raise children effectively, you will want to raise them to know and respect the fire of God's manifest presence. While Eli's story may not make a good basis for a Father's Day sermon, there is something here we all want to take to heart. Just as we wouldn't want asbestos in the ceilings of our homes, we also don't want to allow the asbestos of irreverence into our family life.

INVITING THE FLAMES

There are two ways we can welcome fire. The first is by praying that God will fill our homes with His tangible presence. The second is by cultivating an atmosphere of reverence, or the healthy fear of the Lord.

Praying for God's Presence

Just because my wife and I fear the Lord and desire His presence does not automatically mean our kids will. They have their own personalities and will make their own choices. One day this hit me like an eighteen-wheeler. I was speaking at a youth conference in Ohio, accompanied by one of my four children (I'm not free to tell you which one). I suddenly realized, *This child evidences zero spiritual hunger. There is no indication that this child desires God in any way.*

Startled, I wondered, *Is this my child? How can this be happening?* I asked a thousand questions without much resolution.

I cried a code-blue prayer, and God gave me a few Bible verses that significantly built up my faith. The verses had nothing to do with parenting, but they had everything to do with inviting the fire of God's manifest presence into our home: "When you pray, say . . . your kingdom come,"[7] and "Blessed are those who hunger and thirst for righteousness, for they will be filled."[8] The first verse gave Sherry and me confidence to invite the kingdom of God to come on our child. The second gave us confidence that because spiritual hunger is part of the kingdom of God, we had His permission to pray such hunger into the life of our child. We prayed something like this:

> Father, in the name of the Lord Jesus Christ, we cry out to You on behalf of _____. You have given us the role of praying down the kingdom of God on our child. One

facet of Your kingdom that we are keenly concerned about is our child's hunger and thirst for the things of God. Won't You pour out Your Holy Spirit on _____ and give a deep desire to know Christ, to follow hard after Christ? This is Your Word, and we ask You to do it.

Soon after we began to pray in this way, our child made a public confession of faith in Christ, chose to be water baptized, and began to grow significantly in love with Jesus. Through this process God taught us how to begin praying for the fire of His manifest presence for others, particularly in our own family.

In addition to the verses above, we also rely on Jesus' promise in Luke 11:13: "If you then, though you are evil, know how to give good gifts to your children, how much more will your Father in heaven give the Holy Spirit to those who ask him!" Jesus doesn't limit us to asking the Father to send the Holy Spirit only to ourselves, so my wife and I consistently pray this promise for many in our sphere of influence, including our children and other family members.

Cultivating Reverence

Once we begin to see God manifest His presence in our homes and in our children's lives, a few other steps may help our children develop a reverence for God.

Keep a record of answers to prayer. Some families use a Box of Remembrance to keep letters or other physical objects to remind them vividly of what God did. When our children were little, Sherry and I started a Red-Hot Prayer Book. We recorded our prayers in blue or black ink, and we'd write or underline the answers in red. Our daughter, Andrea, would often say with great joy at the dinner table, "Don't forget to underline that in red! That's what God did. He deserves the credit!" After the first six months, we were amazed at how much red was sprinkled throughout the pages. (Now that I think of it, red makes a good connection with fire!)

Worship together in your home. Encourage every child, in his or her own ways, to participate in a time each week when you sing, read some Bible verses, talk about what is happening in your lives, and pray for each other. Singing to the Lord is one of the most important elements of family worship. If you lack confidence in your own musical abilities, listen to a CD of worship music.

Treat baptism and the Lord's Supper with reverence. Wait to allow your children to take the Lord's Supper until they are well prepared. They should be able to express in their own words what Communion represents and why they personally need the benefits of Christ's sacrifice. I'd also recommend you hold off from permitting your children to be baptized until they have the right understanding and right motives. Postponing a good thing helps to raise the bar of anticipation and makes the baptism more special when it does occur.

Celebrate all spiritual markers, such as water baptism, with as much passion as you celebrate academic or athletic achievements. When your children show spiritual hunger in any way, such as choosing to attend a Bible study or prayer group with peers, affirm them by saying something like, "It is so exciting to see God at work in your life. He must have big plans for you."

Exercise zero tolerance of R- or X-rated videos. Obviously all Internet pornography is off limits. Put filters on your computer. Set the example yourself; it is impossible to cultivate spiritual passion while indulging in a secret pornography habit. When your kids are teenagers, help them look up movie reviews and critiques online and teach them how to discern right from wrong for themselves.[9]

Utilize the power of blessing. There is nothing more powerful than our words of encouragement to our children. We want to call forth the good in our children by saying, when appropriate, "Jesus loves you,"

"God's hand is on your life," "God gave you a strong mind; it's great to see you honoring Him with it."

Leverage family vacations as a time to build spiritual vision in your children. As young parents, Sherry and I learned that it's far better to take a vacation *with* God than to take a vacation *from* God. On vacation, we would memorize a chapter from the Bible, read through a book of the Bible, study a biblical theme, and certainly sing together. (When we sang in the car, the kids called it "car-tunes.") Our children often recall those times: "Remember memorizing Psalm 1 in Maine?" "Yeah, and remember that awesome time in Jackson Hole, when we learned how to listen to God?"

Cultivate humility. Finally, the fire of God's manifest presence is attracted to homes where there is humility. When our spirits are broken, repentant, and contrite, God shows up in a hurry. Humility enables us sincerely to say, "I'm sorry. I was wrong. Will you forgive me?"

HOME FIRES

When you invite God's presence into your children's lives and help them cultivate reverence, there are thousands of ways God will knock on your front door. Let me share some I have experienced.

Desire for God

Our first-born son was a high-school senior and in need of direction in his life. My wife and I prayed earnestly for him, claiming the Bible promise "I keep asking that the God of our Lord Jesus Christ, the glorious Father, may give you the Spirit of wisdom and revelation, so that you may know him better."[10] He came home from school after baseball practice one evening and announced, "Hey, Dad, I'd like to go away for a night with just me and God. Kind of like a date with God."

I was reading the paper at the time and at first didn't think much of his comment.

Fortunately I had recently begun journaling, recording what I heard God say and where I saw Him working. The next morning with my journal open, I thought, *Now let's see, where have I seen God at work lately?* Suddenly I recalled Fred's comment, and I saw God's fingerprints all over it. Because no one seeks after God on his own, the fact that my son wanted to get away on a date with God indicated that God must have put that desire in him.

Personal Holiness

One day our only daughter, Andrea, bounced through the family room with an armload of books. "Hey, Dad, I've been thinking. I'm about to turn sixteen, and I'd like you to give me a Promise Ring for my birthday." Off she went upstairs to hunker down for the evening with her homework.

The significance of those words didn't hit me until the next morning as I was writing in my journal. *Wow! My only daughter wants me to give her a Promise Ring as a symbol of her commitment to moral purity. She wants to remain sexually pure. This is huge. This is God!* Then God said to me, *Get her the ring.* And now I am dedicating this book to her faithful husband!

Radical Commitment

One evening I had arrived home late from work. "Are the kids awake?" I asked Sherry.

"I don't know," she replied, "but go upstairs and check. I know they'd love to see you."

Outside Andrew's door, I called in a loud whisper, "Andrew, you awake?" No answer. But from nine-year-old Stephen's room I heard, "Oh, hey, Dad. How's it going?"

I greeted him, then asked, "Tell me something significant that happened in your life today."

His eyes flashed back and forth as he searched for the right words to express himself. "In chapel they told us all about Stephen in the Bible," he said slowly. He got real serious, and his little chin started quivering. I always know something deep is stirring inside Stephen's spirit when that happens. It's as if his chin and heart are hot-wired together. "Dad, did you know that the first martyr in the early church had the name Stephen, just like me? He was the first person killed because he was a Christian."

By now his chin was really shaking, and his eyes were moist. I will never forget his next words: "Dad, I've decided that someday I'd be willing to die for Jesus too."

Yikes! I thought. *What makes a nine-year-old boy willing to die for Jesus?* He wasn't saying that because his dad is a pastor or because it was the right thing to say. This was God working in my son.

"Stephen," I answered, with tears in my own eyes, "if you ever have the opportunity to die for Jesus, don't miss it! There is nothing that would make your mother and me more proud of you."

This was a holy parenting moment. The manifest presence of God was all over my son. When I left his room, I got alone with God, kneeled in prayer, and thanked Him for working in my son at such a profound level.

Healing Power

We want to see dramatic answers to specific prayers in our homes so that our children know firsthand that God is alive and powerful. That is precisely what happened at the Hartley home one day.

"How was your day?" I asked Sherry when I arrived home.

"Well, it's better now," she answered, explaining that she had suffered with a debilitating headache. "I tried to call you all day to ask you to pray for me, but when I couldn't reach you, I asked Andrew to pray for me." I looked across the room at our six-year-old son smiling from ear to ear.

"I sat down next to him," she continued. "He put his hand on my shoulder and asked God to take away my headache. Almost immediately it disappeared." By now, Andrew's big smile had gotten even bigger. His eyes were shining as he nodded in joyful agreement.

That was better than anything we could have gotten out of a Tylenol bottle. What more do I want my children to experience than the tangible result of their own specific prayers? They don't need long, fancy prayers. But they do need to see results.

Soul Winning

When Fred was fourteen, he hit a home run deep over the center-field fence for his high-school baseball team. It was the first home run by anyone in the new Christian school. What a happy day! I can still remember seeing him running the bases, rounding third, and then planting his foot on home plate to the screams from the stands.

Two years later, he told me that he had prayed with a couple of youth to receive the free gift of eternal life. As I watched him telling his story, the joy on his countenance was greater than it had been when he hit the home run. That's God at work.

Yes, God gives us authority as parents to pray in significant ways for our kids. And as we pray, we are able to see God's manifest presence revealed in their lives.

One of those ultimate questions in family life becomes, *What size flame am I passing on to the next generation?* Bottom line, I cannot light my children's fuses. God is self-revealing and only He can make Himself known. At the same time, we certainly want to open the door to God and expose our children to the fire of His manifest presence.

$\wr$ $\wr$ $\wr$

The fire that God manifests in our homes is also capable of transforming our churches. God's expressed presence is much bigger than me and mine. God's flaming presence shines brighter when His people gather together. If you are tired of playing church, wait until you see what God wants to do right down the middle of your Christian fellowship. The next chapter will give you hope for your church family.

CHAPTER NINE

MY CONGREGATION ON FIRE

No man is greater than his prayer life. The pastor who is not praying is playing; the people who are not praying are straying.
LEONARD RAVENHILL[1]

Wherever one looks in the church today, there is an evident need for a deeper work of the Holy Spirit.
JOHN R. W. STOTT[2]

We are constantly on a stretch if not a strain to devise new methods, new plans, new organizations to advance the church and secure enlargement and efficiency for the Gospel. . . . Men are God's method. The church is looking for better methods; God is looking for better men. . . . The Holy Ghost does not flow through methods, but through men. He does not come on machinery, but men. He does not anoint plans, but men—men of prayer.
E. M. BOUNDS[3]

I am sitting in seat 20A aboard a Delta Air France airplane on a runway at Charles de Gaulle Airport, Paris, waiting to take off on my return flight to Atlanta. I am staring out the window at one of the most massive jet engines I have ever seen. Shaquille O'Neal could easily go one-on-one against Yao Ming inside the thing. As impressive as the engine's size and design is, however, the engine is only as effective as the fuel that feeds it.

I look forward to sitting back for nine hours, reading a good book, catching some Zs, maybe watching a movie. God forbid that somewhere over the Atlantic that monster engine should decide that it doesn't need the fuel anymore. If it gets proud and arrogant and decides it can take us the rest of the way on its own ... uh, well ... that engine and all the rest of us are in for a big surprise. As powerful as the engine looks, it is nothing but dead weight without its fuel and flame.

In the modern church, we have somehow gotten the idea that we can fly without the fuel of God's Spirit and without the fire of God's manifest presence. Some of our congregations have gotten big and impressive, but we have also become proud and self-sufficient.

Ours is the first culture in history to have growing churches and shrinking prayer meetings. Leonard Ravenhill exposed this condition with a broken heart and a flaming pen:

> Poverty-stricken as the church is today in many things, she is most stricken here, in the place of prayer. We have many organizers, but few agonizers; many players and payers, few pray-ers; many singers, few clingers; lots of pastors, few wrestlers; many fears, few tears; much fashion, little passion; many interferers, few intercessors; many writers, but few fighters. Failing here we fail everywhere.[4]

It is no wonder church-growth expert C. Peter Wagner reports that there is not a single county in the United States that is experiencing church growth; all we are doing is shuffling members from smaller churches to larger ones.

Prayer on fire is where we must start. Once we are filled with the Holy Spirit and begin to experience the fullness of God's daily presence in our lives, we want nothing more than for our church to have a fresh encounter with the power of God.

The flame of God's presence is the power cell of the church. Without the conspicuous presence of God, we will never be able to function the way He intended. Our worship, discipleship, fellowship, and outreach all depend on the clear revelation of Christ among us.

So, where do we start corporately in an attempt to get the fire back in our engine? We start corporately the same place we started individually—with God's promise to fill us with His Holy Spirit.

CORPORATE INFILLINGS

When Christ handed the early disciples the promise of the Father— "receive the Holy Spirit"[5]—they obviously heard it correctly: They gathered *as a community* to receive the infilling. Acts 2 records that the entire assembly of believers in the Upper Room were filled corporately.

When the apostle Paul wrote, "Be filled with the Spirit,"[6] he was exhorting believers corporately. The verb *be filled* is plural in the original Greek and clearly communicates, "All of you believers [gathered in the city of Ephesus] are to be filled with the Spirit."

When Paul told the believers in Colosse about "Christ in you, the hope of glory,"[7] he was again speaking to them corporately; the *you* is distinctly plural.

We see this same corporate filling of the Holy Spirit throughout history. In revival after revival, entire assemblies of believers were filled with the Holy Spirit simultaneously.

Given this compelling history, it is difficult for me to understand why so many Christian leaders individualize the filling of the

Holy Spirit. We have been taught to get alone with God, to pray privately, and to deal with God one-on-one. While any of us can apply the biblical principle to our own lives and God will certainly fill us privately, that is not the biblical norm. Our rugged Western individualism has stolen the joy and dynamic of the corporate infilling. Is it any wonder we have trouble sustaining fire in our congregations? Separate the logs and the fire goes out; put them together and watch them blaze.

That's what happened just a hundred years ago in Wales. On a Monday night in 1904, young Evan Roberts met with seventeen youth in Moriah Chapel in South Wales. That night many students trusted Christ as Savior. Roberts taught them to ask, "Send the Holy Spirit now for Jesus' sake." He directed them not to sing, not to tell stories, but simply to pray for one thing: the fullness of the Holy Spirit. Let's allow him to tell it in his own words.

> The people were sitting, and only closed their eyes. The prayer began with me. Then it went from seat to seat— boys and girls—young men and maidens. Some asked in silence, some aloud, some coldly, some with warmth, some formally, some with tears, some with difficulty, some adding to it . . . strong voices, then tender voices. Oh, wonderful! I never thought of such an effect. I felt the place beginning to be filled, and before the prayer had gone half way through the chapel, I could hear some brother weeping, sobbing, saying, "Oh, dear! Dear! Well! Well!" On went the prayer, the feeling became more intense; the place being filled more and more.[8]

Roberts explained that some in the crowd were so overwhelmed by God's presence that they yelled words like, "No more, Lord Jesus, or I'll die!" Some lay face down on the floor. Others wept.

Many sang in joyful celebration. This was only the beginning of a sweeping move of God throughout Wales.[9]

CONGREGATIONS ON FIRE

Reading accounts of God breaking into churches and revealing His presence to His people en masse ignites a desire in us to see Him break into our congregation as well. When He does, our evangelism flourishes, our experience of God's manifested presence changes, and our prayers are empowered.

Evangelism

When God chooses to make Himself known by pouring out His Spirit on His people, they get right with Him and the evangelism that flows out of the church is renewed. Jesus said, referring to the Holy Spirit, "I will send him [the Holy Spirit] to you [the believers]. When he comes [to you, the believers] he will convict the world of guilt."[10] This pattern—the local church encountering the transforming presence of the Holy Spirit, followed by evangelism in the surrounding community—is what my friend Armin Gesswein called "God's Law of Revival."[11] He explained it this way:

- Non-Christian seekers will deal with their sins according to the way Christians first deal with theirs.
- When Christians are filled with the Holy Spirit, non-Christians will be convicted of sin and converted to Christ.
- When Christians wake up (revival), non-Christians will also wake up (evangelism).[12]

Manifestation Gifts

Another prominent way God manifests His presence in church life, as we discussed earlier, is through His spiritual gifts. While we have already considered the biblical explanation of why the manifestation gifts are critical if we are to know the manifest presence of Christ, let me now give an illustration.

My son and I were seated in prayer with 380 African leaders in a room built for 200—at the most. An African friend seated next to me had been quietly translating the prayers for my benefit. Suddenly he stopped translating even though an African pastor was still praying. My discerning son tapped me on the shoulder and asked, "Dad, is that what I think it is?"

"What do you think it is?" I replied.

"Is that the gift of tongues?" he asked. He was right; the pastor was speaking in tongues. Somehow my son knew even though he didn't know any of the languages being spoken. What happened next is nothing short of phenomenal.

We waited for an interpretation. God gave me a word of knowledge regarding who had the interpretation; I handed the microphone to the woman and, through my translator, encouraged her to give the message. With deep contrition and holy trembling, she spoke a prophetic word that cut like a knife to the core of the people's spirits. Virtually everyone in the room groaned and wept. Some screamed in desperation and repentance as God revealed His holy presence to the group. There were other prophecies and healings of various kinds. A deaf man could hear. A woman suffering from malaria fever was instantly healed. Five hours of nonstop repentance followed. God had used the manifestation gifts to lead His people to a fresh encounter with the risen Christ.

Corporate Prayer

When the Holy Spirit is present in a church, perhaps the most obvious result is that people begin to pray together.

At a moment of deep passion when Christ wanted to identify the proper phrase to describe the gathering together of God's people, He proclaimed, "My house will be a house of prayer."[13] He could have chosen many other names: House of Preaching, House of Song, House of Covered-Dish Dinners, House of Evangelism, House of World Missions, House of Small Groups. All these are good things, but they were not good enough to be named as the predominant activity that is to characterize the gathering of believers. It is as if God says to us, *When My people gather together, My presence should be so conspicuous that there will be no guessing. And the single activity that will attract My tangible presence to your gatherings is prayer.*

What we discover from Pentecost is that prayer brings the flaming presence of the Holy Spirit, and the Holy Spirit in turn sustains fire-attracting prayer. Though this sounds like circular reasoning, it is not. Remember that we can't want God unless He first puts the desire in us. God prompts us to pray for His presence as a means of preparing us to receive His presence. Spurgeon had it right:

> The condition of the church may be very accurately gauged by its prayer meetings. So is the prayer meeting a grace-ometer, and from it we may judge the amount of divine working among a people. If God be near a church, it must prayer. And if He be not there, one of the first tokens of His absence will be a slothfulness in prayer.[14]

When I pastored my first church in Homestead, Florida, south of Miami, I worked like a dog. I wanted to be a successful pastor. I wanted to make my church grow, even if it killed me. And it almost did. One night my wife had to call 911 because I had severe chest pains and my heart was racing. An ambulance rushed me to the hospital where a cardiologist diagnosed me as suffering from a wicked case of heartburn and battle fatigue. The heartburn was caused by the onion rings and Coke I'd had at midnight; the battle fatigue was from working too hard and praying too little. I repented and began a prayer journey that night. When my family and I arrived in Atlanta seventeen years ago, God put me in a vice grip of prayer and built prayer into my life and ministry from the ground up.

STEPPING OUT

While this book is a biblical theology of encountering the manifest presence of God in prayer, I'd also like to share some steps you can take to see your church filled with God's flaming presence.

- Pray for your church to be brought to a crisis infilling of the Holy Spirit. Just as you personally received the infilling of the Holy Spirit by faith, cup your hands and receive His infilling as a member of your congregation, praying, *"Holy Spirit, I know that You desire to fill our congregation; please start with me. I am confident that I am not the only hungry God-seeker in our church family. Give all of us an increased passion for a fresh encounter with You."* As you pray, you may want to use the Bible verses listed in appendix 1.
- Gather a small group of God-seekers from your church fellowship and pray with them each week for a corporate filling of the Holy Spirit. Keep your eyes open for new people to join your prayer group, particularly those you might not suspect. You will learn that the movers and shakers in the kingdom of God are not necessarily the movers and shakers in society. A useful tool you may use to determine people's sense of desperation is found in appendix 2.
- If you are a pastor, preach messages on a regular basis about how to be filled with the Holy Spirit. At the end of your message, give people the opportunity to receive the infilling.

- If you are not the pastor, volunteer to be a personal intercessor for your pastor. If your church does not have a team of people who pray for the pastor, organize one, praying for Holy Spirit anointing for your pastor and for the entire church.
- Volunteer to teach a Bible class on the Holy Spirit or on revival prayer. This book may be a helpful resource.
- Attend a Prayer Summit.[15] Invite others to join with you.
- Ask God to activate the manifestation gifts in your life and in your church family. Step out. Be bold in prayer. Ask God for miracles in your church family that will attract unusual attention to God.
- Volunteer to start a prayer committee. Just as a church has a missions committee or finance committee, your pastor would most likely appreciate a team of faithful prayer mobilizers.
- Set up a prayer room where members can pray during the Sunday worship for what is happening in the service.
- Work toward establishing a weekly, churchwide, worship-based prayer rally. Even if you start small, start somewhere.

This list includes quite a few steps, and you shouldn't tackle them all at once. Ask the Holy Spirit how to begin. He is an effective pastor. He loves your church fellowship, and you can trust His leadership and initiative. The Holy Spirit is not about to force His way into your Sunday-morning worship. However, He is eager to draw you into a fresh encounter with Christ. He has just the key to open your congregation to His manifest presence, and He will tell you where to start.

God has His own plan for your church. The reason I did not

share more specifics from my own church ministry is to avoid suggesting a formula. One size does not fit all when it comes to leading a congregation into a fresh encounter with God. Listen to the Holy Spirit; He knows and loves your church fellowship more than you do.

$$\xi \quad \xi \quad \xi$$

The fire of corporate prayer is not limited to our church. Something powerful happens when we link arms with believers from other fellowships. As we will discover, there are some blessings Christ is withholding from us until we join together on a broader scale. Have you ever heard of backdraft?

CHAPTER TEN

BACKDRAFT

*Spiritual awakening: When the Father wakes us up to see
Christ's fullness in new ways, so that together we trust Him,
love Him, and obey Him in new ways, so that we move with
Him in new ways for the fulfillment of His global purpose.*
DAVID BRYANT[1]

*I long for more and more to be filled with the Spirit, and to see
my congregation move and melt under the Word, as
in great revival times, "the place shaken where they are
assembled together," because the Lord has come in power.*
ANDREW BONAR[2]

Backdraft is a firefighter's worst nightmare.

Here's how it happens. Fire requires three elements: fuel, heat, and oxygen. Under certain conditions when a building is on fire, oxygen gets sucked out of a room to fuel fire raging elsewhere. This leaves plenty of super-heated fuel in the room, but no oxygen. If a firefighter breaks a window, puts his ax through a door, or somehow introduces oxygen back into the room, the result is a major explosion of fire. The phenomenon is called backdraft.

All over the world God is calling together small groups of God-seekers who are praying for the fresh fire of His presence. What we are asking for is a form of holy backdraft. We want God to saturate us with the fuel of His Holy Spirit, heat our hearts into white-hot desperation, and then at the right moment, introduce the third and critical element. When God breathes on us His breath of life . . . backdraft! Some call this explosion of God's presence "revival."

We've looked at what happens when God manifests His presence to us personally and in our church. But He wants to do even more by working in geographical areas, across denominational lines.

UP CLOSE AND PERSONAL

Tasting the manifest presence of God for ourselves is both hunger-satisfying and hunger-inducing. On the one hand, there is nothing in the entire world our souls long for like spending moments feasting our eyes on the glory of God in the face of Christ; just one look is radically transforming and refreshingly fulfilling. We know at once that this splendor is what we were made for. On the other hand, we want more. That first glance immediately ignites a healthy passion that is not easily satisfied. This hunger for more leads us to want to link arms with brothers and sisters in the broader body of Christ and to cry out to God for a wider outpouring of His Holy Spirit.

Over the past fifteen years I have been blown away as I've watched masses of people throughout the world gather in revival prayer. For example, I was part of the Atlanta Global Day of Prayer on Pentecost Sunday, May 15, 2005. While I joined with six thousand believers in the Philips Arena, an estimated 200 million people were meeting in 156 countries in virtually every time zone around the globe. As many as 25 million believers were praying from the African continent alone. And we were all praying for a fresh Pentecost. This means that on the same day, one out of every thirty-two people on earth were crying out to God for a fresh outpouring of His Holy

Spirit![3] We are certainly safe to say that things around the globe are heating up.

Perhaps you are wondering, *This is all so big; what does it have to do with me?* Or you may be asking, *Where can I plug in?*

I can assure you that it has everything to do with you, because I fully believe that what God has in store for His church is so big that it will affect all of us. I am also confident that He is inviting not only me, but you as well, to be part of a mighty move of His Holy Spirit. Regarding where to plug in, we will get to several specific steps you can take. But first, we want to lay the biblical and historic framework for expecting God to move in this way.

COMING FIRE

"Backdraft" can be written over the second chapter of the book of Acts. Though I have frequently referred to the Upper Room, what the 120 believers experienced there is not only a powerful example of prayer on fire, it also illustrates the vital role of corporate prayer in the activity of God. The early church had been praying for ten days. God was soaking them in the oil of His Holy Spirit. Their hearts were heated in holy desperation, knowing that without the empowerment of the risen Christ they were doomed to failure.

They heard a rumble off in the distance. As they listened, the sound got louder. As they worshiped and prayed, it grew more emphatic. The next thing they knew was holy backdraft: Fire erupted, hearts were cleansed, lives were transformed. The inward-focused band was filled with God's holy presence and turned inside out. There is no way to contain such a raging inferno. They ran outside, and those in the streets heard the explosion and demanded answers.

Cowardly Peter, who had denied Christ three times, instantly became courageous Peter and preached a Christ-manifesting message.

On that day, three thousand Jews put their faith in Jesus their Messiah. There is only one viable explanation for what happened. The explosion of God's presence affected them individually, it affected them corporately, and it dramatically affected the community. Rather than destroying life, Holy Spirit backdraft transforms life. Backdraft has been the hope of God's people throughout history, and it is our hope today.

The fire God wants to send to my city of Atlanta is bigger than any First Baptist or Second Methodist or Third Presbyterian Church could possibly contain. When God pours out His flaming presence, every congregation—the Pentecostal Holiness Church down the street, the Congregational and the Vineyard churches across town, the Lutherans, the Nazarenes, and the Salvationists—will experience a noticeable increase in Holy Spirit activity.

When God said, "I will pour out my Spirit on all people,"[4] He promised backdraft. The Hebrew prophet Zechariah saw this backdraft moment from a distance and licked his lips in anticipation.

> This is what the LORD Almighty says: "Many peoples and the inhabitants of many cities will yet come, and the inhabitants of one city will go to another and say, 'Let us go at once to entreat the LORD and seek the LORD Almighty. I myself am going.' And many peoples and powerful nations will come to Jerusalem to seek the LORD Almighty and to entreat him."
>
> This is what the LORD Almighty says: "In those days ten men from all languages and nations will take firm hold of one Jew by the hem of his robe and say, 'Let us go with you, because we have heard that God is with you.'"[5]

Obviously Zechariah is describing something far bigger than a parochial brushfire. This is something pervasive and ongoing. People from surrounding nations and from various language groups are getting wind of it and making a trek to see for themselves. Urgency is in the air; they want to travel "at once." The blaze is obviously prayer-driven, because they identify their purpose as "to seek the LORD Almighty and to entreat him." And make no mistake about it; this massive people movement is all driven by the power cell of the manifest presence of God. "We have heard that God is with you," the seekers say. The flame of God's name is driving this revolution.

Some theologians think this massive turning to God will be a single moment in church history, and others see it as a process. Whichever group is right, we all certainly want to see the Holy Spirit sweep through the church.

A LOOK IN THE REARVIEW MIRROR

As we look at where the church has been, we see countless moments along the road of history as the landscape was set ablaze with the presence of God.

- On New Year's Day 1739, John and Charles Wesley, George Whitefield, and a band of seventy others met at Fetter Lane in London. "About three in the morning, as we were continuing instant in prayer, the power of God came mightily upon us, insomuch that many cried out for exceeding joy, and many fell to the ground (overcome by the power of God). As soon as we recovered a little from that awe and amazement at the presence of His majesty, we broke out with one voice, 'We praise thee, O God; we acknowledge thee to be the Lord.'"[6] This moment is known as the Methodist Pentecost.
- New York State was ablaze with God's presence in August 1825. When Charles Finney walked into a large cotton mill outside of Utica, a girl working a loom looked into his eyes and began trembling. Her shaking

fingers snapped the thread and operations halted. The girl next to her looked up to see what had happened. As she saw Finney's face, she was also affected. In one person after another, conviction of sin spread throughout, and the looms all stopped. By the time the owner arrived to investigate, the entire workforce was in tears. He wisely ordered work to cease and gave his employees opportunity to respond to Christ. Up until that moment, Finney had not said a word.[7]

- Off the northwest coast of Scotland, the rugged Hebrides Islands received a remarkable outpouring of God's Holy Spirit in 1828. "O God, I seem to be gazing through an open door. I see the Lamb in the midst of the throne," one fifteen-year-old youth cried in public prayer. "O God, there is power there, let it loose!" That's all it took. The floodgates of heaven suddenly opened. People were sobbing, lying on the floor, begging for mercy.

  As the revival spread, prayer meetings lasted twenty-four hours. Hundreds of people in various villages begged to be saved. At times the presence of God was so tangible at the close of a worship service that the organists were literally unable to move their hands over the keyboards.[8]

- In 1858, the *Washington National Intelligence*, a leading newspaper, reported that daily prayer meetings were held in 150 towns in Massachusetts, 200 in New York, 60 in New Jersey, 65 in Pennsylvania, and 200 in Ohio. It is estimated that, of the United States population of thirty million, nearly two million were born again during this remarkable move of God's Holy Spirit.[9]

- In 1859 the landscape of Northern Ireland was ablaze with God's presence. This movement started in First Presbyterian Church. The pastor reported, "The meeting fell still as a grave; the stillness was fearful. Those present will never forget it. At length the silence was broken by unearthly cries, uttered simultaneously by several in different parts of the church. . . . [People] lay in mental agony and absolute bodily prostration." Out of this deep conviction and repentance came a robust movement of emblazoned God-seekers. At seven o'clock every evening in the town of Derry, a public prayer meeting was held at Corn Market. Between five hundred and five thousand would gather for three hours each night.[10]
- In December 1904, New York and New Jersey again experienced a dramatic move of God's Spirit. City newspapers published daily columns entitled "The Fires of Pentecost," "Yesterday's Conversions," and "The Power of Prayer." In Atlantic City, with a population of 6,000 people, 5,950 were reportedly born again. One article reported, "Pentecost was literally repeated . . . spacious churches crowded to over-flowing, and great processions passing through the streets."[11]
- On February 3, 1970, in Wilmore, Kentucky, Asbury College experienced a fire-visitation of God. The college dean had dedicated that day's chapel service to student testimonies. Soon it was obvious that God was calling the students to a fresh encounter. One after another, students confessed sin with gut-wrenching honesty, transparency, and rock-bottom repentance. When the bell sounded to dismiss for class, no one left

the building. Not for class, not for lunch, dinner, or bedtime. God was in the room and time stood still. Nearly every seat in the 1,550-seat auditorium was full for 144 hours of heaven on earth.[12]

- I have saved my favorite example of backdraft for last. On May 13, 1727, the Holy Spirit visited a band of Christians in Herrnhut, Germany. "The whole place was indeed a veritable dwelling of God with man," wrote their godly pastor, Count Nicholas Ludwig von Zinzendorf.

At six years of age, Zinzendorf had thrown love letters to Jesus from the window of his castle. As a youth, he was trained in Franke's school in Halle, where he founded the Order of the Mustard Seed, a missionary prayer band, among his peers. From there he studied at Wittenberg, where he led all-night prayer meetings. "I have but one passion—'tis He and He only," he would say. As an adult, Zinzendorf invested his resources in building a community for three hundred Moravian believers with whom he shared a common passion. Together they formed Herrnhut, or "the Lord's Watch," a praying fellowship with a mission to reach a lost world through a revived church.

After weeks of concerted prayer, on May 13 they received their "baptism with the Holy Spirit." Love, obedience, fellowship, and prayer abounded. Prejudice, secret estrangement, and misunderstandings were exposed and put away. "Signs and wonders were seen among us, and there was great grace on the whole neighborhood." The entire congregation bowed under a sense of God's presence and continued in prayer until midnight. Children were changed. By August 22, the community established an around-the-clock prayer meeting, appointing a man and a woman to be "in the Lord's Watch" at all times. Each person would serve at their watch one hour each week.

Soon people in neighboring communities learned of the move of God's Spirit and likewise came under profound conviction and repentance. The ripples spread as far as Turkey, Morocco, and Greenland. Within five years the community sent out their first missionaries. Over the subsequent years, they sent out six hundred teams of missionaries.

J. R. Mott and others attribute this Herrnhut Pentecost as the birthplace of the modern missionary movement. This means that the hundreds of thousands of missionaries who have been sent out over the past 275 years owe a little of their thrust to this 24/7 prayer meeting that lasted one hundred years.[13]

A LOOK OVER THE HOOD

It is encouraging to look back at how God has used the backdraft principle to ignite revivals throughout history. But what God is doing in our day to prepare His people for a massive outpouring of His Holy Spirit is even more engaging.

- Leading demographer David Barrett reports that 170 million Christians worldwide are currently praying daily for a spiritual awakening and global evangelism.[14] George Otis Jr. observes, "About seventy percent of all prayer toward completing the Great Commission has taken place since 1900. Of that, seventy percent has occurred since World War II. And seventy percent of that has come about in the 1990s alone!"[15] In other words, prayer and missions are heating up.

- The church worldwide is facing increased persecution. In the 1980s, 270,000 died every year as Christian martyrs. It is currently estimated that as many as 500,000 people are martyred every year.[16] We can say that spiritual zeal is heating up.
- In India, an estimated 15,000 new believers are being baptized every week, 80 percent of whom are responding to Christ because of a supernatural out-of-the-box encounter. In China, 25,000 are coming to Christ every day. Thirty-six percent of the population of the Commonwealth of Independent States (formerly the Soviet Union) are believers in Christ. In the great African continent, 20,000 are now coming to Christ every day. The evangelical church in Latin America is growing three times faster than the population. And more Muslims have come to Christ in the past decade than in the previous one thousand years.[17] Clearly, world evangelism is heating up.

Christian leaders are noticing and affirming what God is doing in our day:

- Dr. Paul Cedar, past president of the Evangelical Free Church in America and former president of the National Association of Evangelicals said, "Without a doubt, the major opportunity before us is the potential of an historic revival akin to the first and second great awakenings which took place in the early history of the United States."[18]
- Bill Bright, founder of Campus Crusade for Christ, the largest world missionary force, said before his death,

"Wherever I go I sense a God-given conviction that revival is desperately needed. Lately I have sensed that the Body of Christ is on the verge of the greatest spiritual break-through in the history of Christianity."[19]

- Christian theologian and philosopher Os Guinness wrote, "There will be a massive revitalization of American life, including both its ideals and institutions, through a movement of decisive spiritual revival and reformation."[20]

- When he was the United States Senate chaplain, Richard Halverson said, "I believe we're on the threshold of something happening that is going to be as great or greater than the Reformation."[21]

- Dr. James Dobson, founder of Focus on the Family, wrote in response to the moral disintegration of our society, "What can we do? What should be our response? First, we must continue to pray for worldwide revival that will reawaken millions of people spiritually."[22]

- While speaking to three thousand leaders from 150 nations at the Lausanne Congress on World Evangelization, Billy Graham said, "I believe as we approach the latter days it could be a time also of great revival . . . a rain of blessings, showers falling from heaven upon all the continents before the coming of our Lord."[23]

According to the temperature gauges of our Christian leaders, the atmosphere of holy anticipation is certainly heating up.

INSIDE THE BUS

We've seen how God has moved explosively in the past and how God is building hope to see yet another explosive move in our day. What does this have to do with you and me? How can we share in such a massive move of God?

Well, let me assure you that you are not just a spectator along for the ride. You may not feel important, but you have a strategic role to play. Allow me to get specific. The following four action steps are known as prayer rhythms. Just as every area of healthy life has rhythms—the daily cycles of sleep, the earth's rotation, the ocean's tidal movements, the four annual seasons—so a healthy spiritual life enjoys a similar cadence.

1. Each day receive a fresh filling of the Holy Spirit. When we personally receive the filling of the Holy Spirit, we have a portion of that widespread move of God toward which we are praying. For backdraft to occur corporately, it is vital for us to be filled individually. Learn to use the Bible promises of fire as you pray (see appendix 1).

2. Gather weekly with a small group of like-minded people and pray for a broad outpouring of the Holy Spirit. Our own spiritual zeal is fanned with brothers and sisters of common passion. If you don't know of such a group, start one. And don't be afraid to start small. Once God shows up, "small" becomes an irrelevant concept. The important rule is to be consistent—generally that means gathering every week. Less often than that is usually inadequate for maintaining focus.

3. Gather quarterly across racial and denominational lines with area congregations for prayer rallies. Normally these gatherings include pastors, intercessors, and marketplace Christian leaders. Ask your pastor about them and encourage your congregation to participate.

4. Once a year on the National Day of Prayer (the first Thursday in May) as well as on the Global Day of Prayer (Pentecost Sunday) gather with the broader body of Christ in your city. God seems to withhold some blessings from us until we climb out of our individualism and link arms with believers from each corner of the larger church. On the final night of His life, Christ prayed that we might be one—that we might experience the relational unity that is supernaturally accessible to all who profess faith in Christ's resurrection.[24]

Could it be that Christ is heating up His church in preparation for one massive backdraft? Evangelical scholar J. Edwin Orr, who spent sixty years of research acquiring three earned doctorates in the study of spiritual awakenings, summarized in one simple statement all he had learned "Whenever God is ready to do something new with his people, He always sets them to praying."[25] You and I are living in such a day when God is indeed doing something new.

When the massive outpouring of God's Spirit for which we have prayed takes place, perhaps we will remember the word *backdraft*.

ʆ   ʆ   ʆ

So where does prayer on fire take us? If it has its desired effect, where does it lead us? And how will we know when we get there? Now that we have seen what prayer on fire is and how it works, we are ready to consider where we are going.

CHAPTER ELEVEN

CHRIST ON FIRE

*Everything in Christ astonishes me! Neither history, nor
humanity, nor the ages, nor nature, offer me anything with
which I am able to compare him and by which I am able to
explain him. Here is everything extraordinary.*
NAPOLEON BONAPARTE[1]

*Jesus is my God, Jesus is my Spouse, Jesus is my Life.
Jesus is my only Love, Jesus is my All, Jesus is my Everything.
Because of this I am never afraid. I am doing my work
with Jesus. I am doing it for Jesus. I am doing it to Jesus;
therefore, the results are his, and not mine.*
MOTHER TERESA[2]

Prayer on fire takes us to Jesus. It exalts Christ to His rightful position of supremacy over all things. When we experience the manifest presence of God, we come to know Christ in all His fullness.

The sad reality is that for too long we have settled for a shrunken
Christ—an undersized, anemic, economy model of Christ. Stephen
Prothero makes some strong comments about the American Jesus:
"In the United States, Jesus is widely hailed as the King of kings. But
it is a strange sort of sovereign who is so slavishly responsive to his
subjects. . . . The American Jesus is more a pawn than a king, pushed

around in a complex game of cultural chess, sacrificed here for this cause and there for another."[3]

When we worship an undersized Jesus, we have pews full of people who know about Christ but whose hearts have yet to be touched by His flame. Christian psychologist Larry Crabb wrote insightfully,

> Unbelievers do not see Christ as their greatest Treasure. Neither do most believers. We live as blind people, chasing after the light we can see—the satisfaction that blessings bring—and not valuing the light we cannot see—the Glory of Christ. More is available to us in Christ than we dare imagine. We settle for so much less. We taste Him so little.[4]

My good friend David Bryant describes this distorted understanding of Jesus as "a crisis of Christology." This crisis is probably less a theological issue than an experiential one. The problem is not that preachers are actually teaching heresy about Christ. We believe that Christ is God, all right; but do we treat Him that way? We still believe in His second coming, but do we act as if it will happen any time soon? We believe in His lordship, but do we allow it to affect our lifestyles? We believe that He answers prayer, but what are we tangibly receiving from Him?

A shrunken, undersized Jesus will never change my life, let alone transform my community. An impoverished, austere Christ will never mobilize the church to triumphantly reach the final unreached peoples of the world. And is it any surprise that we stop praying when we have such a dwarfed view of Jesus? If Jesus is so small and incompetent, we might as well forget about prayer and make the best of things on our own.

God's answer to this crisis of Christology is prayer on fire. If we want to see Christ assume His rightful place of supremacy, we must embrace God's manifest presence.

"LORD, SET ME ON FIRE"

You will recall the request my son-in-law, Josh, made of me: "Can you pray that the Lord would set me on fire?" I hear in his request the heart cry of a God-seeker who is tired of playing church and longs for spiritual reality. I hear the resolve of one who knows the *source* of fire is not from within himself, but is exclusively in God.

I hear the desperation of one who knows the *need* for fire. He is weary of pushing the right buttons and jumping through the hoops without experiencing the full blessing of Christ in his life and ministry.

I hear the passion of one who knows that prayer is the *primary precursor* to the fire of God's manifest presence. He knows that God does not toss fire in arbitrary directions but sends it intentionally to those who wholeheartedly seek Him—and so Josh has asked me to pray specifically for him.

The cry of "Lord, set me on fire" expresses a desire for a fresh encounter with Christ. All the ways God manifests Himself—in our inner lives, in our families, in our congregations, and in our communities—bring us to a fresh encounter with the risen Christ.

The apostle Paul wrote, "For God, who said, 'Let light shine out of darkness,' made his light shine in our hearts to give us the light of the knowledge of the glory of God in the face of Christ."[5] This means that whenever God chooses to manifest Himself, His revelation always leads us to see the light of the knowledge of the glory of God in the face of Jesus Christ.

Paul explained the identity of Christ to believers in the Turkish city of Colosse this way: "He is the image of the invisible God."[6] The word translated image is the Greek word icon, from which we get "idol." As believers we know that idolatry is wrong. However, Jesus is not a false idol; He is the genuine thing—the spittin' image of His Father. When God shows Himself to us, it is always in Christ. The author of Hebrews wrote, "The Son is the radiance of God's glory and the exact representation of his being."[7]

Jesus said of the Holy Spirit, "He will testify about me."[8] In other words, "He will brag about Me and He will never stop bragging about Me. He's my cheerleader." Jesus went on to say, "He will bring glory to me."[9] It was another way of saying, "The Holy Spirit puts the spotlight on Me and He keeps the spotlight on Me so that I remain center stage."

LOOK AT JESUS

Now that you and I have encountered Christ in the flames of God's manifest presence, even the way we read the Bible changes. As John Armstrong said:

> The whole Bible is focused on Jesus Christ, from Genesis to Revelation. Revival will come only when we as God's people return to the supremacy of Jesus Christ. Recovering the wonders of "Christ alone" is not merely an antiquated slogan from the 16th Century Reformation Period. It is the flame which will ignite a new reformation today.

It is fair to say that when God manifests His flaming presence, He puts *everything* in its proper place.

- *He puts Christ in His proper place.* Most significant, when God manifests His conspicuous presence, Christ assumes His position of supremacy over all things and is acknowledged as the King of kings and Lord of lords.

- *He puts us in our proper places.* As we have discovered, once we encounter the manifest presence of God, for the first time we see ourselves for who we really are, and we can step into the destiny for which we were created.
- *He puts the devil in his proper place.* When the flames of God's tangible presence are revealed, demons tremble and the powers of darkness are pushed back.

British theologian John R. W. Stott said, "The riches of Christ are unsearchable. Like the earth, they are too vast to explore, like the sea too deep to fathom. They are untraceable, inexhaustible, ill-limitable, inscrutable and incalculable. What is for certain about the wealth Christ has and gives, is that we should never come to an end of it."[10]

Perhaps Josh's heart cry is echoing in your soul as well. Perhaps you would love to see God torch your inner life with a holy zeal. "Can you pray that the Lord would set me on fire?" is the cry of a God-seeker who passionately longs for all there is in Christ. As Jacob wrestled all night with God in prayer and would not let Him go until God blessed him, God is placing in His people a tenacity for His fullness. They are like the people the psalmist wrote of: "Such is the generation of those who seek him, of those who seek your face, O God of Jacob."[11]

Such God-seekers know the *nature* of fire. When they cry, "Set me on fire," they know a fresh encounter with God is personal, overpowering, invasive, and risky. They want more from their prayer life than baby food and leftovers. They want more from their daily devotions than a five-minute warm fuzzy and a pat on the back. They want the molten lava of God's blazing, all-consuming presence. Far more important than learning theories about fire, they want to be touched. Consumed. Purified. Filled. Empowered. You show me someone who has been filled with the Holy Spirit, and I will show you someone head over heels in love with Jesus Christ.

When Josh and those like him say, "I have one request," they are not kidding. They know this is an ultimate, winners-take-all request. With a prayer request like this, they only *need* one request. This prayer leads them to the mother lode. When God answers this prayer, in one way or another, He meets all other needs simultaneously.

This band of seekers has the *hope* of fire. The very fact that Josh would ask me to pray for such a thing—and that you would read a book on this subject—shows that hope is already alive in him and in you. Hope of coming fire is the first deep work God does when He prepares a people for fire. The beauty of hope is that "hope does not disappoint us, because God has poured out his love into our hearts by the Holy Spirit, whom he has given us."[12] Once we receive the infilling of the Holy Spirit, God's love is infused into our spirits at such an infectious level that we desire more of God. What we have already received is a portion of what we are still praying. What we have encountered personally, we long to see the broader body of Christ experience as well.

Finally these pray-ers are learning that the *object* of our fire is Christ. We recognize in Him all we long for, and we worship Him for all He's worth. When the Holy Spirit takes hold of our prayer lives, we too will see the blazing splendor of Christ. Prayer on fire is God's way to bring us into intimacy with Jesus.

The cry for God to set us on fire is expressed well by Charles Spurgeon. Though his words below were originally prayed more than 150 years ago, they still bubble with vitality today.

> O God, send us the Holy Spirit! Give us both the breath of spiritual life and the fire of unconquerable zeal. You are our God. Answer us by fire, we pray to you! Answer us both by wind and fire, and then we will see you to be God indeed. The Kingdom comes not, and the work is

flagging. Oh, that you would send the wind and the fire! And you will do this when we are all of one accord, all believing, all expecting, all prepared by prayer.[13]

This is what God desires—a unified, faith-filled, prayer-energized people who are brimming over with hope, to whom He is preparing to send a sweeping, consuming, empowering move of His Holy Spirit so that Christ might receive His due. Saint Patrick, the great fifth-century missionary to Ireland, said it this way:

Christ be with me, Christ within me,
Christ behind me, Christ before me,
Christ beside me, Christ to win me,
Christ beneath me, Christ above me,
Christ in quiet, Christ in danger,
Christ in hearts of all that love me,
Christ in mouth of friend and stranger.

Can you pray that the Lord would set me on fire? Yes, I can. I have. And I will.

I pray it for Josh and for me and for you. I pray it for my church in Lilburn, Georgia, and for the city-church in Atlanta. I pray for fire because it is clearly God's will; there is nothing He wants more. I pray for God to lead us to a fresh encounter with the risen Christ. I pray it and I receive right now a portion of that toward which I am praying.

By now we should understand that *prayer on fire* is the single, most critical issue facing the church today. It is, after all, nothing short of a fresh encounter with the risen Christ that will transform my life and my family, energize my church, mobilize my mission, and ultimately reach the final unreached peoples of the world. We dare not settle for anything less. Nothing short of fresh fire will consume the wood, hay, and stubble of our feeble self-made efforts and kindle the holy, get-it-done-at-any-cost zeal in us. The precursor to Christ's return will be a church that is ablaze with first-love passion for Christ and His kingdom.

To experience *prayer on fire* is to be consumed with Jesus. Have at it!

FIRE STARTERS

God's Answer for the Lukewarm Heart
(Promises to Pray Back to God
for His Manifest Presence)

The Fire of Answered Prayer

The god who answers by fire—he is God. (1 Kings 18:24)

Father God, send Your flaming presence into my prayer life today. Take the dry tinder of my inner life and show Yourself to be the God who answers by fire.

The Fire of His Fullness

Do not get drunk on wine, which leads to debauchery. Instead, be filled with the Spirit. (Ephesians 5:18)

Father, I receive right now by faith the infilling of Your Holy Spirit in the name of the Lord Jesus Christ. Saturate every area of my life, every cell in my body with Your holy presence. Take control of me—spirit, soul, and body.

The Fire of His Thirst-Quenching Presence

On the last and greatest day of the Feast, Jesus stood and said in a loud voice, "If anyone is thirsty, let him come to me and drink. Whoever believes in me, as the Scripture has said, streams of living water will flow from within him." (John 7:37-38)

Father, I am thirsty. Dry. Parched. Because You give me permission to partake, I come and drink deeply from You. I receive now from the overflowing fountain of Your Holy Spirit. Fill every area of my life to overflowing with Your dear presence.

The Fire of His Empowerment

"But you will receive power when the Holy Spirit comes on you; and you will be my witnesses in Jerusalem, and in all Judea and Samaria, and to the ends of the earth." (Acts 1:8)

Father, I freely admit that apart from You I can do nothing. Today I receive a fresh outpouring of Your Holy Spirit. And I receive the empowerment to be Your witness in every sphere You open to me.

The Fire of His Holy Spirit

"If you then, though you are evil, know how to give good gifts to your children, how much more will your

Father in heaven give the Holy Spirit to those who ask him!" (Luke 11:13)

Father, more than asking, today I receive Your Holy Spirit for myself and for those in my sphere of influence . . . [be specific].

The Fire of His Love

And I pray that you, being rooted and established in love, may have power, together with all the saints, to grasp how wide and long and high and deep is the love of Christ, and to know this love that surpasses knowledge— that you may be filled to the measure of all the fullness of God. (Ephesians 3:17-19)

Father, baptize me afresh in Your love. Immerse me. May the love of Christ conspicuously permeate my life so that others might see more of Him and less of me.

The Fire of His Righteousness

Sow for yourselves righteousness, reap the fruit of unfailing love, and break up your unplowed ground; for it is time to seek the LORD until he comes and showers righteousness on you. (Hosea 10:12)

Father, I do take hold of You today until You come and shower righteousness down on me and my people. Father, it is time to seek the Lord. As I am seeking, I am believing You to be showering.

The Fire of His Face

May God be gracious to us and bless us and make his face
shine upon us, that your ways may be known on earth,
your salvation among all nations. (Psalm 67:1-2)

Shine, Jesus, shine! Fill this land with Your blazing pres-
ence. Take the veil off our eyes as we gaze on the noonday
sun of Your glory. We want the nations to be drawn to
Your salvation.

The Fire of New Clothes

"I am going to send you what my Father has promised; but
stay in the city until you have been clothed with power
from on high." (Luke 24:49; see also Acts 1:4)

Father, I am tired of being unclothed. Today I put on the
new clothes of Your Holy Spirit power. You have promised
them to me. They fit perfectly. May they draw attention to
You all day long.

The Fire of His Imminence

Come near to God and he will come near to you.
(James 4:8)

Father, as I intentionally approach You today, won't You
conspicuously approach me? Please don't be subtle.
Tangibly manifest Your presence right down the middle
of my life.

The Fire of Hope

May the God of hope fill you with all joy and peace as you trust in him, so that you may overflow with hope by the power of the Holy Spirit. (Romans 15:13)

Father, I do trust You with all that I have and all that I am. Now fill me with all the joy and all the peace You have for me. Flood my soul with such supernatural hope that it sloshes around, brims over, and affects those in my sphere of influence.

The Fire of Repentance

Repent, then, and turn to God, so that your sins may be wiped out, that times of refreshing may come from the Lord. (Acts 3:19)

Father, I receive the gift of repentance. May it do its good work in me and in those around me so that You can rid the landscape of sin, that a season of Holy Spirit refreshment might come.

The Fire of His Fellowship

"Here I am! I stand at the door and knock. If anyone hears my voice and opens the door, I will come in and eat with him, and he with me." (Revelation 3:20)

Father, more than an occasional visit, I genuinely long for Your living-room presence. I throw open wide the front

door of my life to You. Please come in and make Yourself
right at home. From now on my home is Your home.

The Fire of Preparation

A voice of one calling: "In the desert prepare the way
for the LORD; make straight in the wilderness a highway
for our God. Every valley shall be raised up, every
mountain and hill made low; the rough ground
shall become level, the rugged places a plain." (Isaiah
40:3-4)

Father, I welcome Your demolition in my life and among
Your people. Tear down the prideful high place; remove
the boulders of selfishness; straighten out my deceitful
ways; raise up the humble, the lowly, and the contrite. We
want to be a six-lane highway so You can ride into town.

The Fire of the Knowledge of His Glory

For the earth will be filled with the knowledge of the glory
of the LORD, as the waters cover the sea. (Habakkuk 2:14)

Father, today Your glory is already covering the earth,
but what I want to see is the knowledge of the glory of the
Lord covering the earth. I don't want Your presence to go
unnoticed by anyone.

The Fire of His Prayer Life

In the same way, the Spirit helps us in our weakness. We
do not know what we ought to pray for, but the Spirit

himself intercedes for us with groans that words cannot express. (Romans 8:26)

Father, there is no sense pretending. You know the impotence of my prayer life. You promise to pray for me and in me, so that Your prayer life becomes my prayer life. I trust You to keep that promise in me now as I pray.

The Fire of His Revelation

I keep asking that the God of our Lord Jesus Christ, the glorious Father, may give you the Spirit of wisdom and revelation, so that you may know him better. (Ephesians 1:17)

Father, You don't force Your presence on any of us. You are far too gracious for that. Instead You send Your Holy Spirit to give wisdom into who You are in principle and revelation into who You are in reality. Come on me and my people [be specific] *so that we might have a desire to know You better and better and better.*

URGENCY SURVEY

This survey from David Bryant's book *The Hope at Hand* is a great tool to use in your fellowship group to evaluate people's sense of desperation.[1]

1. To what extent does the church worldwide (including our church) need a greater manifestation of all that Christ is for us, in us, and through us? To what degree are we in need of a true biblical revival?

1	2	3	4	5	6

It would be helpful, but not essential to our task.

Without it most churches (our own included) will languish, and we will fall short of God's purposes for us in this generation.

2. What impact would a world revival (as well as revival where we live) have on the worldwide advance of Christ's kingdom? To what degree is revival in the church the only hope for our city and for the nations?

1	2	3	4	5	6

It would be helpful, but not essential to our task.

We can never carry out the Great Commission task to the comprehensive degree that God has called us to in this generation without a true biblical revival.

3. How strategic is it for the body of Christ (including our church) to work concertedly in prayer and preparation for a coming world revival?

1	2	3	4	5	6

It would be helpful, but not essential to a local and worldwide revival.

God will respond with a local and worldwide awakening in the church only if we unite as a body to pray for it and to prepare for it together.

4. Is God willing, able, and ready to give world revival to this generation (and to us right here)?

1	2	3	4	5	6

Undoubtedly, God is able. I'm not sure He wants to at this time.

Absolutely! God yearns to do such a thing right now. It is His highest priority for us in this generation.

5. Does God desire to fill His church (including our church) with confidence and hope about a coming revival and to enable us to seek it and prepare for it together?

1	2	3	4	5	6

I'm not sure.

Absolutely! Such a spirit of corporate hope and obedience is a gift of God.

6. Am I ready to get involved right now with other believers in new ways to seek and prepare for local and world revival?

1	2	3	4	5	6

I'm not sure.

I want to make such involvement a number-one priority in my life, reflected in such things as my commitments of time, energy, resources, and prayer.

STUDY GUIDE QUESTIONS

Chapter 1: God On Fire

1. Rate the fervency of your prayer life (1 = ice cold; 10 = ablaze with the presence of God).
2. Rate the fervency of the prayer life of your church.
3. Give some characteristics of a lukewarm heart. A lukewarm church.
4. What is the difference between human passion and the fire of God?
5. How is the omnipresence of God different from His manifest presence?
6. Why would the author suggest that "Lord, teach us to pray" is a watershed prayer?

Chapter 2: A Biblical Theology of Fire

1. What does it mean to say that God is on fire?
2. Which Bible account of God's fire stood out to you? In what way?
3. Why would the author say that God's Word is on fire?
4. Of the examples of what happens when God's people are on fire, which have you experienced personally? Which have you observed in the lives of others? Give examples.
5. What does it mean for an individual Christian to be referred to as a "flame-bearer"?

Chapter 3: Holy Spirit Fire

1. Why is there so much controversy about the Holy Spirit?

2. Which of the seven facts about the Holy Spirit impressed you most? Why?
3. Tell in your own words what it means to be filled with the Holy Spirit. How would the author define being filled with the Holy Spirit?
4. When the author describes his experience of being filled with the Holy Spirit, what strikes a chord with you?
5. How do you see evidence in your own life of hunger for God?

Chapter 4: Filled with Fire

1. What healthy characteristics did you see in the two men from North Carolina?
2. How are you treating the Holy Spirit? Since He lives inside of you and you are constantly relating to Him one way or another, describe that relationship in your own words.
3. Respond to this statement: "Spiritual hunger reveals spiritual health."
4. Why is it imperative that we know for certain that we are filled with the Holy Spirit?
5. What evidence of being filled with the Holy Spirit is obvious in your life?

Chapter 5: Fire in the Prayer Closet

1. What does Romans 8:26 tell us about overcoming prayerlessness?
2. This is where the rubber meets the road. Specifically, in what ways does the Holy Spirit bring reality into our prayer lives? Which of these have you experienced? Which would you like to experience?
3. What does it mean to "pray in the Spirit"?
4. What does it mean to pray with cupped hands? How could you begin to do so?

Chapter 6: Out of the Box

1. Describe the box of naturalism in your own words. In what spheres of life do you see its influence? Be specific.
2. Describe a person who is theoretically a supernaturalist, but who is in reality a practicing naturalist. How does accepting one view mentally but living and praying differently affect his or her life with God?
3. What does it mean to take the lid off the box and climb out?
4. In what ways can our theology box God out?
5. What does "touching the fire" refer to? How does this demonstrate the sin of irreverence?
6. Give examples of how Jesus lived outside every box.

Chapter 7: Ashes

1. Have you ever encountered God in a way that produced in you a broken and contrite spirit? Has He ever reduced you to ashes?
2. How did Molly and John demonstrate brokenness?
3. Can you give an example of someone you know who demonstrates an ongoing ashen spirit?

Chapter 8: Keeping the Home Fires Burning

1. What are some ways we can hinder the flame of God in our homes?
2. In what ways can we fan the flame of God's presence in our homes?
3. Have you ever recognized the dreaded asbestos of irreverence in your own heart or in the lives of your children? How did it show itself?
4. What would it look like to pray down God's presence into your family? Have you ever experienced this presence? What did it look like?

Chapter 9: My Congregation On Fire

1. In what way would your church change if God were to show up? Be specific.
2. As you were reading the examples from history of churches that caught fire with God's presence, what are some of the characteristics you should look for in your own?
3. What would you love to see God do in your church?
4. What are some practical steps you can take to be instrumental in seeing your church catch fire?

Chapter 10: Backdraft

1. In your own words, define spiritual backdraft.
2. Which example of historical backdraft impressed you the most? Why?
3. What is a common thread connecting the great revivals in history?
4. Discuss the following statement by J. Edwin Orr: "Whenever God is ready to do something new with His people, He always sets them to praying."
5. What evidence is there today that God may be preparing His church for a massive outpouring of the Holy Spirit? Do you see any of this evidence in your community?

Chapter 11: Christ On Fire

1. What does the author mean when he says, "Prayer on fire takes us to Jesus"?
2. Do you agree that the modern church is facing a crisis of Christology? What evidence do you observe that supports your view?

3. What motivates a believer to pray, "Lord, set me on fire"? Be specific. What would characterize the life of one in whom God answers this prayer?
4. Do you agree with the following statement: "Prayer on fire is the single, most critical issue facing the church today"? Why or why not?

NOTES

Introduction
1. See Genesis 15.
2. See Exodus 3.
3. See Exodus 19.
4. See Exodus 13.
5. See 1 Chronicles 21:26.
6. See 2 Chronicles 7.
7. See 1 Kings 18.
8. See Isaiah 6.
9. Matthew 3:11.
10. See Acts 2.
11. Acts 9:5.
12. 1 Thessalonians 5:19.
13. See Revelation 1.
14. Hebrews 12:29.
15. V. Raymond Edman, *They Found the Secret* (Grand Rapids, MI: Zondervan, 1984), 29.
16. Edman, 52.
17. A. Skevington Wood, *The Burning Heart* (Minneapolis: Bethany Fellowship, 1978), 59.
18. Wesley Duewel, *Revival Fire* (Grand Rapids, MI: Zondervan, 1995), 56.
19. http://en.wikipedia.org/wiki/John_Calvin
20. Elisabeth Elliot, *Shadow of the Almighty* (Grand Rapids, MI: Zondervan, 1958), 58.
21. Charles Spurgeon, *The Soul Winner* (Scotland: Christian Focus Publications, 1993), 99.
22. Charles Spurgeon, "A Mournful Defection—John 6:67," from *Spurgeon's Sermons,* electronic database. Biblesoft, 1997.
23. Charles Spurgeon, "Camp Law and Camp Life—Deut. 23:14," from *Spurgeon's Sermons,* electronic database. Biblesoft, 1997.

24. Jim Cymbala, *Fresh Wind, Fresh Fire* (Grand Rapids, MI: Zondervan, 1997), 182.
25. Matt Redman, "I Need to Get the Fire Back," © 1996 Thankyou Music.
26. Matt Redman, "Worship Flame,"© 2004 Thankyou Music.
27. Darin Sasser and Jason Harrison, "Light a Fire in Me," © 1998 Shadow Rock Music.
28. Tim Hughes, "Consuming Fire," © 2002 Thankyou Music.
29. "Sending," Charlie Hall, Nathan Nockels, and Stuart Townsend, © 2003 worshiptogether.com.
30. "Consuming Fire," Johnny Mac Powell, Dan Avery, David Carr, Mark Lee, and Sam Anderson, © 1995 Class Reunion Music.
31. See Jeremiah 29:13.

Chapter 1: God On Fire
1. Erwin Raphael McManus, *An Unstoppable Force* (Orange City, CA: Flagship Church Resources, 2001), 176–178.
2. C. S. Lewis, *The Chronicles of Narnia* (Great Britain: HarperCollins, 2001), 146.
3. Deuteronomy 4:24; Hebrews 12:29.
4. Gary McClure, "Top Ten Issues Facing Today's Church," *Pray!*, July/August 2005, 10. For this article, McClure conducted a survey of 1,300 evangelical leaders from virtually every segment of the church: Southern Baptist and an array of other Baptists, Assembly of God, Roman Catholic, Presbyterian, Methodist, Nazarene, Church of Christ, and Christian Church. The LifeWay study revealed emphatic results.
5. Revelation 3:16.
6. Revelation 3:20.
7. Romans 3:11-18.
8. See Luke 11:1,2-4,5-8,9-12.
9. Luke 11:13.
10. For a twelve-week study in how Jesus trained His disciples to pray, see Fred A. Hartley III, *Lord, Teach Us to Pray* (NavPress, 2003).
11. Romans 8:26.
12. Ephesians 6:18.
13. A. W. Tozer, *The Pursuit of God* (Camphill, PA: Christian Publications, 1982), 60.

14. Tozer, 60.
15. Tozer, 61.
16. See www.collegeofprayer.org

Chapter 2: A Biblical Theology of Fire

1. Leonard Ravenhill, *Why Revival Tarries* (Minneapolis: Bethany Fellowship, 1959), 111.
2. E. M. Bounds, *The Necessity of Prayer*, http://www.worldinvisible.com/library/bounds/5bb.10596-necessity%20of%20prayer/5bb.10596.04.htm, accessed January 10, 2006.
3. Ravenhill, 62.
4. In a real sense, the first of God's creative works was to make fire: "And God said, 'Let there be light,' and there was light" (Genesis 1:3). Because light is the release of energy by fire, when God uttered His first recorded words, He essentially said, "Let there be fire." Neon, incandescent, fluorescent, magnesium, quartz, or halogen? Who knows. What we do know is that He gathered combustible gases into a critical mass, fire was created, and light resulted.
5. "By the same word the present heavens and earth are reserved for fire, being kept for the day of judgment and destruction of ungodly men" (2 Peter 3:7).
6. Gerhard Kittel, *Theological Dictionary of the New Testament*, vol. 6 (Grand Rapids, MI: Eerdmans, 1964), 935.
7. Deuteronomy 4:24, Hebrews 12:29.
8. Exodus 19:18-19.
9. Exodus 19:12.
10. Hebrews 12:28-29.
11. See John 1:14,18; Colossians 1:15; Hebrews 1:1-3.
12. See Revelation 1:14-16. In addition, John describes the flaming altar, flaming angels, flaming plagues, and flaming fireballs from heaven.
13. John 9:5.
14. John 1:4.
15. See Revelation 21:23.
16. Matthew 3:11.
17. See Acts 2:1-3.
18. 1 Thessalonians 5:19.
19. Jeremiah 23:29.

20. See Jeremiah 20:9.
21. See Jeremiah 5:14.
22. See Ezekiel 1:4,13,27.
23. See Ezekiel 10:6; 16:41; 23:47; 28:14,16; 30:8,14; 39:6.
24. See Daniel 10:6.
25. See Hosea 8:14.
26. See Joel 2:3.
27. See Obadiah 1:18.
28. See Micah 1:4.
29. See Nahum 1:6; 3:13,15.
30. See Zephaniah 1:18; 3:8.
31. See Zechariah 2:5.
32. See Malachi 3:2.
33. Luke 24:32.
34. See Luke 24:27.
35. Acts 2:3-4.
36. See Ezekiel 1:28; Acts 2:37; Isaiah 6.
37. See Isaiah 6:1-7.
38. See Isaiah 66:15.
39. Kittel, vol. 6, 937.
40. For example, see the account of Sodom and Gomorrah in Genesis 19. This incident is on the most-misunderstood-Bible-stories shortlist. "How could a loving, compassionate God do such a cruel and destructive thing?" people ask. When the account is read in full, we realize that God's acid rain was the only merciful, compassionate thing He could have done. Genesis 18:20-21 discloses the otherwise missing ingredient. Countless innocent victims were crying out to God for vengeance. As we read with this in mind, the real question becomes, "How could a loving, compassionate God do anything other than step in?" The image of judgment fire and a coming day of reckoning when God will once again manifest Himself in purifying fire is repeated throughout the Old Testament. See Leviticus 10:2; Numbers 11:1-3; 16:35; and 2 Kings 1:10.
41. See Leviticus 1:1.
42. Leviticus 6:12.
43. Exodus 30:8.
44. See Revelation 5:8.

45. Psalm 141:2.
46. Revelation 5:8.
47. See Eugene Peterson, *Reverse Thunder* (San Francisco: Harper, 1988).
48. Moses, like many of God's great leaders, received his call from the fire (see Exodus 3). When the smoke cleared, what had changed in Moses' world? He was no longer a domineering vigilante who would kill an unruly Egyptian with his bare hands (see Exodus 2); he was soon to become the meekest man on the face of the earth (see Numbers 12:3). According to the writer of Hebrews, Moses' radical change came because when he met God in the fire, he was actually introduced to the preincarnate Christ (see Hebrews 11:26).
49. Abraham, see Genesis 15:17; David, see 1 Chronicles 21:26; Solomon, see 2 Chronicles 7:1; Isaiah, see Isaiah 6; Ezekiel, see Ezekiel 1:4.
50. See Acts 1–2.
51. See Matthew 28:19; Acts 1:4; Luke 24:49; Acts 1:8.
52. See Acts 1:14-15.
53. See Luke 24:49; Acts 1:4-5.
54. Acts 1:8.
55. Acts 1:14.
56. Acts 2:2.
57. Acts 2:5.
58. See Acts 2:9-11.
59. Acts 2:38-39.
60. Acts 2:39.
61. See Revelation 1:20.
62. 1 Corinthians 12:7.
63. Walter Bauer, William F. Arndt, and F. Wilbur Gingrich, *A Greek-English Lexicon of the New Testament* (Chicago: The University of Chicago Press, 1957), 860.
64. Matthew 5:14,16.

Chapter 3: Holy Spirit Fire

1. Andrew Murray, *The Full Blessing of Pentecost* (Old Tappan, NJ: Revell), vii.
2. Matthew 3:11.
3. 1 Thessalonians 5:19.
4. See Acts 2:3.

5. See Matthew 3:16; John 7:37-39; 20:22; Matthew 3:11.
6. See Romans 15:30; Ephesians 4:30; Hebrews 10:29.
7. See 1 Corinthians 12:11; Acts 21:11 and Ezekiel 11:5; Acts 16:6-7; 8:29; Romans 8:14.
8. See John 14:26; Romans 8:16; 8:27; 1 Corinthians 2:10-11.
9. See Acts 13:2; John 16:8-11.
10. See John 14:16-17; 16:7-14.
11. R. A. Torrey, *The Holy Spirit* (Old Tappan, NJ: Revell, 1977), 11.
12. See Genesis 1:3,6,9,14,20,24; Colossians 1:16-17; Genesis 1:2.
13. See Luke 1:26-35.
14. Romans 8:9.
15. Philippians 2:13.
16. Romans 8:26.
17. Ephesians 6:18.
18. O. Hallesby, *Prayer* (Minneapolis: Augsburg, 1931), 170.
19. John 3:8.
20. Leonard Ravenhill, *Why Revival Tarries* (Minneapolis: Bethany Fellowship, 1959), 112.
21. John 15:26; 16:14.
22. Ephesians 5:18.
23. Ephesians 3:19.
24. Colossians 2:9-10.
25. See Romans 8:9.
26. See Acts 2:38-39; Ephesians 5:18.
27. See Ephesians 5:18; Colossians 2:9-10.
28. See Acts 2:38-39; Ephesians 5:18.
29. See Galatians 3:2-3.
30. See Philippians 3:8-9; Psalm 42:1-2.
31. See Matthew 5:6; John 7:37-38.
32. See Galatians 5:22-26; Acts 1:8.
33. Ephesians 5:18.
34. See Ephesians 5:18; John 7:37-38; Acts 2:38-39.
35. John 7:37-39.
36. Ephesians 5:18.
37. Luke 11:13.
38. Acts 1:8.

Chapter 4: Filled with Fire

1. R. A. Torrey, *Why God Used D. L. Moody* (Old Tappan, NJ: Revell, 1923), 56.
2. 1 Kings 18:24.
3. See Acts 7:51; Hebrews 10:29; Acts 5:3; Mark 3:28-30; Ephesians 4:30; 1 Thessalonians 5:19.
4. Luke 11:13.
5. John 7:37-38.
6. See John 20:22.
7. Ephesians 5:18.
8. Psalms 63:1.
9. Philippians 3:10,13-14.
10. Ephesians 1:17.
11. A. W. Tozer, *How to Be Filled with the Holy Spirit* (Harrisburg, PA: Christian Publications, 1991), 42.
12. See John 20:22.
13. Galatians 3:2.
14. Romans 15:29.
15. Luke 24:49; Acts 1:4; 2:38-39.
16. V. Raymond Edman, *They Found the Secret* (Grand Rapids, MI: Zondervan, 1960), 65.
17. The account as recorded by Torrey: "I shall never forget the 8th of July, 1894, to my dying day. It was the closing day of the Northfield Students' Conference—the gathering of the students from the eastern colleges. Mr. Moody had asked me to preach on Saturday night and Sunday morning on The Baptism with the Holy Ghost. On Saturday night I had spoken about 'The Baptism with the Holy Ghost, What it is, What it does, the Need of it and the Possibility of it.' On Sunday morning I spoke on 'The Baptism with the Holy Spirit, How to Get It.' It was just exactly twelve o'clock when I finished my morning sermon, and I took out my watch and said: 'Mr. Moody has invited us all to go up on the mountain at three o'clock this afternoon to pray for the power of the Holy Spirit. It is three hours to three o'clock. Some of you cannot wait three hours. You do not need to wait. Go to your rooms, go out into the woods, go to your tent, go anywhere where you can get alone with God and have this matter out with Him.' At three o'clock we all gathered in front of Mr. Moody's mother's house (she was then

still living), and then began to pass down the lane, through the gate, up on the mountainside. There were four hundred and fifty-six of us in all; I know the number because Paul Moody counted us as we passed through the gate.

"After a while Mr. Moody said: 'I don't think we need to go any further; let us sit down here.' We sat down on stumps and logs and on the ground. Mr. Moody said: 'Have any of you students anything to say?' I think about seventy-five of them arose, one after the other, and said: 'Mr. Moody, I could not wait till three o'clock; I have been alone with God since the morning service, and I believe I have a right to say that I have been baptized with the Holy Spirit.' When these testimonies were over, Mr. Moody said: 'Young men, I can't see any reason why we shouldn't kneel down here right now and ask God that the Holy Ghost may fall upon us just as definitely as He fell upon the apostles on the Day of Pentecost. Let us pray.' And we did pray, there on the mountainside. As we had gone up the mountainside heavy clouds had been gathering, just as we began to pray those clouds broke and the rain-drops began to fall through the overhanging pines. But there was another cloud that had been gathering over Northfield for ten days, a cloud big with the mercy and grace and power of God, and as we began to pray our prayers seemed to pierce that cloud and the Holy Ghost fell upon us. Men and women, that is what we all need—the Baptism with the Holy Ghost." Torrey, 57–59.

18. See 1 John 1:9.
19. See Romans 5:1-5.
20. Tim Stafford, "The Pentecostal Gold Standard," *Christianity Today,* July 2005, 28.

Chapter 5: Fire in the Prayer Closet

1. Leonard Ravenhill, *Why Revival Tarries* (Minneapolis: Bethany Fellowship, 1959), 19.
2. David Wells, (lecture, Hamilton, Mass., Gordon-Conwell Theological Seminary, October 1979).
3. Romans 8:26.
4. Ephesians 6:18.

5. Ephesians 6:18, RSV.
6. Acts 13:3.
7. Dr. Henry Blackaby and his son Richard wrote a helpful book on learning to develop a listening ear to the Spirit of God, *When God Speaks* (Nashville: LifeWay Press, 1995).
8. Ephesians 6:17.
9. Revelation 2–3.
10. Romans 8:14.
11. See Romans 8:9.
12. See Romans 8:13.
13. See Acts 1:8.
14. See 2 Corinthians 3:18.
15. John 5:19.
16. John 17:4.
17. See Luke 6:12-13.

Chapter 6: Out of the Box

1. Elisabeth Elliot, *Through Gates of Splendor* (Grand Rapids, MI: Zondervan, 1958), 44.
2. Andrew Murray, *Key to the Missionary Problem* (Fort Washington, PA: Christian Literature Crusade, 1979), 88.
3. 2 Timothy 3:5.
4. Jack Deere, *Surprised by the Power of the Spirit* (Grand Rapids, MI: Zondervan, 1993), 13.
5. www.Thruthebible.org. Accessed October 18, 2005.
6. R. T. Kendall, *The Sensitivity of the Spirit* (Lake Mary, FL: Charisma House, 2002), 37.
7. See Exodus 7–8.
8. See Acts 8:18.
9. See 2 Thessalonians 2:9.
10. See 1 Corinthians 12,14.
11. See R. T. Kendall, *The Anointing: Yesterday, Today, Tomorrow* (Lake Mary, FL: Charisma House, 2003), xv, xvi.
12. Leviticus 10:1; Numbers 3:4; 26:61.
13. John 5:19.
14. John 14:12.

15. Hebrews 11:6.
16. Dr. Henry Blackaby, *Experiencing God* (Nashville: Lifeway Press, 1990), 108–161.
17. Hebrews 12:2, KJV.
18. Mark 11:23-24.
19. See Matthew 13:58.
20. See Luke 7:9.
21. *Intercessors for America Newsletter,* January 1976.

Chapter 7: Ashes

1. Elisabeth Elliot, *Through Gates of Splendor* (Grand Rapids, MI: Zondervan, 1958), 58–59.
2. Leonard Ravenhill, *Why Revival Tarries* (Minneapolis: Bethany Fellowship, 1959), 106.
3. Isaiah 66:15.
4. See Isaiah 6.
5. Luke 5:8.
6. See Acts 2.
7. See Revelation 1:17.
8. Isaiah 57:15.
9. Psalm 51:17.
10. See Isaiah 61:3.
11. V. Raymond Edman, *They Found the Secret* (Grand Rapids, MI: Zondervan, 1960), 25–33.

Chapter 8: Keeping the Home Fires Burning

1. Dr. Fish is professor of Evangelism at Southwestern Baptist Theological Seminary, where he teaches on awakenings and the history of revival. Quoted in Malcolm McDow and Alvin L. Reid, *Fire Fall: How God Has Shaped History Through Revivals* (Nashville: Broadman, 1997), 319.
2. Richard Owen Roberts, *Revival* (Wheaton, IL: Tyndale, 1983), 65.
3. Bill Gothard, (lecture, Pastor's Conference, Tampa, Florida, Spring 1982).
4. Ephesians 5:18,22,25; 6:1,4.

5. 1 Samuel 2:17.
6. 1 Samuel 4:21-22.
7. Luke 11:2.
8. Matthew 5:6.
9. www.pluggedinonline.com is a good resource. For more insight on this topic see Fred Hartley, *Parenting at Its Best* (Grand Rapids, MI: Revell, 2003).
10. Ephesians 1:17.

Chapter 9: My Congregation On Fire

1. Leonard Ravenhill, *Why Revival Tarries* (Minneapolis: Bethany Fellowship, 1959), 23.
2. John R. W. Stott, *Baptism and Fullness: The Work of the Holy Spirit Today* (Downers Grove, IL: InterVarsity Press, 1964), 13.
3. E. M. Bounds, *Power in Prayer* (Chicago: Moody Press, 1911) 9.
4. Ravenhill, 23.
5. John 20:22.
6. Ephesians 5:18.
7. Colossians 1:27.
8. D. M. Phillips, *Evan Roberts* (London: Marshall Brothers, Keswick House, 1923), 239–240.
9. For the full and glorious report, see H. Elvet Lewis, G. Campbell Morgan, I. V. Neprash, *Glory Filled the Land* (Wheaton, IL: International Awakening Press, 1989).
10. John 16:7-8.
11. For the complete authorized biography of Armin Gesswein, the man who started Billy Graham's prayer ministries, see Fred A. Hartley III, *Everything by Prayer* (Harrisburg, PA: Christian Publications, 2001).
12. Hartley, 27–28.
13. Luke 19:46.
14. Tom Carter, *Spurgeon at His Best* (Grand Rapids, MI: Baker, 1988), 155. Selection from 1873 edition of *Metropolitan Tabernacle Pulpit*, 218.
15. International Renewal Ministries facilitates Prayer Summits throughout North America and around the world. www.prayersummits.net

Chapter 10: Backdraft

1. David Bryant, *Concerts of Prayer* (Ventura, CA: Regal Books, 1984), 40.
2. Andrew Bonar, *Bonar's Diary*, December 13, 1880. Reprinted by *Banner of Truth*, 1991.
3. For more up-to-date information, see www.transformationafrica.com.
4. Acts 2:17; Joel 2:28.
5. Zechariah 8:20-23.
6. John Telford, *The Life of John Wesley* (New York: Hunt & Eaton, n.d.), 117.
7. Wesley Duewel, *Revival Fire* (Grand Rapids, MI: Zondervan, 1995), 103.
8. Andrew Woolsey, *Duncan Campbell* (London: Faith Mission, 1974), 115-135.
9. J. Edwin Orr, *The Fervent Prayer* (Chicago: Moody, 1974), 18.
10. Ian R. K. Paisley, *The "Fifty-Nine" Revival* (Belfast: The Free Presbyterian Church, 1958), 101–102.
11. J. Edwin Orr, *The Flaming Tongue* (Chicago: Moody, 1975), 70–81.
12. Robert Coleman, *One Divine Moment* (Old Tappan, NJ: Revell, 1970), 74–80.
13. Andrew Murray, *Key to the Missionary Problem* (Fort Washington, PA: Christian Literature, 1979), 47–65.
14. David Barrett, *Our Globe and How to Reach It* (Birmingham, AL: New Hope, 1990), 27.
15. George Otis, *The Last of the Giants* (Grand Rapids, MI: Chosen Books, 1991), 144–146.
16. "Martyrdom: The Most Potent Factor in World Evangelism," *Pulse magazine*, July 7, 1989, 5.
17. David Bryant, *The Hope at Hand* (Grand Rapids, MI: Baker Books, 1995), 219–229.
18. *NAE Action*, March–April 1992, 55–56.
19. Worldwide Challenge, March 1983, 29. He made a similar statement with increasing frequency.
20. *Christianity Today*, May 17, 1993, 51. Quoted in David Bryant, *The Hope At Hand* (Grand Rapids, MI: Baker, 1995) 28.
21. Richard Halverson, "On the Threshold of Something Wonderful," *Eternity Magazine*, March 1984, 24–26.

22. Dr. James Dobson, *Focus on the Family,* October 1991, 3.
23. Billy Graham, "The King Is Coming," *Let the Earth Hear His Voice* (Minneapolis: World Wide Publications, 1975), 1466.
24. See John 17:20-26.
25. David Bryant, *The Hope at Hand,* 30–31.

Chapter 11: Christ On Fire

1. David Bryant, *Christ Is All!* (New Providence, NJ: New Providence Publishers, 2004), 77.
2. Bryant, 246.
3. Bryant, 195.
4. Bryant, 203.
5. 2 Corinthians 4:6.
6. Colossians 1:15.
7. Hebrews 1:3.
8. John 15:26.
9. John 16:14.
10. Bryant, 25.
11. Psalm 24:6.
12. Romans 5:5.
13. David Bryant, *The Hope at Hand* (Grand Rapids, MI: Baker, 1995), 61.

Appendix 2: Urgency Survey

1. David Bryant, *The Hope at Hand* (Grand Rapids, MI: Baker, 1995), 182–184. Used with permission (contact www.DavidBryantDirect.com).

AUTHOR

Fred A. Hartley III is the lead pastor of Lilburn Alliance Church and a Christian leader in metro-Atlanta. He and his wife, Sherry, have four children. Fred has been involved in the prayer movement around the world and is the founding president of the College of Prayer International. He is gifted to lead people into a fresh encounter with God. His hobbies include running, riding his motorcycle, playing with his grandchildren, and enjoying a very mediocre game of golf.

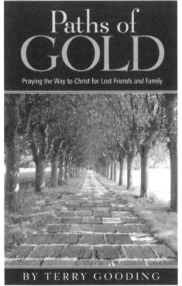

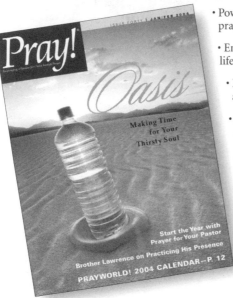